To Frances &

with admiration & affection,

Dick

*The Resurgence of the West*

# *The Resurgence of the West*

## How a Transatlantic Union Can Prevent War and Restore the United States and Europe

RICHARD ROSECRANCE

Yale UNIVERSITY PRESS

New Haven & London

Yale University Press books may be purchased in quantity for
educational, business, or promotional use. For information, please
e-mail sales.press@yale.edu (U.S. office) or sales@yaleup.co.uk
(U.K. office).

Set in Janson type by Integrated Publishing Solutions.
Printed in the United States of America.

*Library of Congress Cataloging-in-Publication Data*
Rosecrance, Richard N.
The resurgence of the West : how a transatlantic union can prevent war
and restore the United States and Europe / Richard Rosecrance.
p. cm.
Includes bibliographical references and index.
ISBN 978-0-300-17739-8 (alk. paper)
1. United States—Foreign economic relations—European Union
countries. 2. European Union countries—Foreign economic
relations—United States. I. Title.
HF1456.Z4E856 2013
337.7304—dc23     2012048822

A catalogue record for this book is available from the British Library.

This paper meets the requirements of ANSI/NISO Z39.48–1992
(Permanence of Paper).

10 9 8 7 6 5 4 3 2 1

To Barbara

# Contents

# Contents

# Introduction

The problem we confront is by now familiar. The United States faces a turning point: its long rise is shifting to economic and political decline. The consequences of this decline may well be to speed up a power transition that could bring on a new world war.

Throughout the nineteenth and twentieth centuries the United States routinely triumphed in its economic, political, and military endeavors. Victory over Great Britain in the War of Independence was followed in the mid–nineteenth century by expansion and then consolidation of the American union in the Mexican and Civil Wars. As the nation acquired more people and territory, the greater economic demand in turn released energies to build the railroads and tame the West. American rates of economic development transcended Europe's. By 1890 the U.S. economy was as large as Germany's and England's put together and, indeed, the largest in the world. A host of inventions by Samuel F. B. Morse, Thomas Edison, Alexander

Graham Bell, and others laid the foundation for rapid development of new industries and new communities. These innovations also stimulated federal and state governments along with private enterprise to build the infrastructure—roads, power stations, and telephone lines—that would link the inventions together. The motor car replaced the horse, the telephone replaced the telegraph, and electrification raced from city to countryside. Water and sewage systems made life cleaner and safer from disease, and indoor heating followed. Roads were paved and smoothed to facilitate automobile travel. Heating oil and natural gas supplanted coal-fired furnaces in homes. My parents lived through the last of these changes, and they were amazed at the rapid transformation in their own and their children's lives. My grandfather, who could bring his horse to rest for the night simply by riding her into the barn, found it relatively complicated to perform the same task with his car: that action required steering, braking, and turning the motor off. American inventiveness continues to make communications, text delivery, and picture and TV transmission ubiquitous by successively smaller hand-held devices. Tiny mobile platforms have replaced the larger but more limited desktop machine and office of the past.

Yet the technological and industrial base on which these inventions rest has been slowly eroding. American business does a smaller proportion of the manufacturing sequence, while others produce and ship new devices from China, Japan, Korea, and Taiwan.

Countries that acquire new industrial functions grow rapidly. Rising nations now triple the average U.S. growth rate of 3 percent. After World War II, Germany and Japan achieved

10 percent growth for a decade. China and India are likely to show similar results for several generations because their rural populations have yet to become middle class. Their rapid growth can continue until well into the twenty-first century. The increasing rigidity and truculence of U.S. government institutions also slows America down. Accustomed to repeated international victories and a high level of social services, Americans do not work well together. They ask what their country can do for them, not what they can do for their country. Partisan politics trumps national needs and vision. Crises facing the nation lie unmet as Americans elevate present consumption and personal spending above saving for their and their children's future.[1] The government is equally profligate. As a result, the U.S. government spends when it should save, intervenes too cavalierly abroad, and postpones needed tax increases. America sits numb when it should sense catastrophe.

Europe, growing only 1 percent per year, is in its own way equally passive and neglectful. Unless these halves of the West can come together, forming an even greater research, development, consumption, and financial whole, they will both lose ground. Eastern nations, led by China and India, will surpass the West in growth, innovation, and income—and ultimately in the capacity to project military power.

The United States cannot compensate by raising its rate of growth. A mature economy with an established middle-class population cannot sustain double-digit growth rates over a long period of years. Increased immigration would help because it would raise demand and add workers, but by itself it will not solve America's problems or those of the West as a whole. What should the United States and Europe do to remain relevant in a world that is rapidly shifting to the east with all the economic and possibly military consequences that then might flow? This book seeks to answer that question.

Through the historical mists, I can see two diverging roads. One takes the United States away from economic and political connections with other nations in an effort to solve its severe economic and financial problems in isolation. As we shall see, if the United States chooses this path, it will lose economic, political, and ultimately military momentum. As one Eastern country after another surpasses America in economic strength, the risk of war between the newcomers and the United States increases. Historically, "hegemonic transitions" between leading countries have generally involved major conflict. To take the classic example, Thucydides claimed it was the "growing power of Athens" and the fear that it inspired in Sparta that caused the Peloponnesian War. In the late nineteenth century and the early years of the twentieth, Imperial Germany achieved economic superiority over Great Britain, creating frictions that ultimately led to World War I—a war that at the time was widely considered "inevitable." In the future, a transfer of leadership from an old hegemonic power (America in this case) to a new one could again lead to large-scale violence. The road of isolation leads to the dissipation of American economic and military power and inevitably to the end of the U.S. role as primary leader of the international system.

The alternative, a road less traveled, requires America to recognize that in a partly closed global system that is too large for any nation to encompass or control, even the largest and most powerful nation cannot survive alone. If the United States is to match Eastern gains, it must achieve larger size by joining a more comprehensive economic and political community.[2]

This means the United States must enter a customs union with other Western countries to find enlarged opportunities for trade and growth. The United States has already negotiated free-trade pacts with Canada, Mexico, Colombia, Panama, and South Korea. The formation of a Western economic union with Europe will transform the economic environment, redoubling investment and growth. It will also entail greater cooperation among its member states.[3] A political link with Europe will unblock arteries of trade and investment, rejuvenate the West, and bind it together as did the creative jolt of the Marshall Plan and the NATO treaty during the Cold War. The binding-together we need now, however, is more comprehensive, more daring, and more lasting.

The leaders of the two largest European powers at the World Economic Forum at Davos in January 2012 proposed such an agglomeration of power. Chancellor Angela Merkel of Germany has urged joining the European Union with the United States. French leaders also want closer relations with America, the nation that received France's gift of the Statue of Liberty in 1886. A new economic union of Europe and America would unite 800 million consumers and embrace the most important markets in the world. It would bring 259 of the Fortune 500 largest companies together. The European Union's GDP of $17 trillion is already larger than the $15 trillion of the United States: together they would represent more than half of world GDP, which is currently $61 trillion. Their potent market, research, and development hubs are unmatched. Most of the world's industries based on economies of scale are located in the West or in Japan (which is closer now to the United States than to Eastern nations). If the West comes together, China, India, and other emerging countries will eventually need to link with it in order to maintain their own growth. The magnetic bonds of economic advantage would draw the great powers of the world increasingly together. War would become an outmoded response to the surging forces of technology and globalization.

Such a change would require a profound transformation in American international relations. The U.S. tradition of limited cooperation with most nations but deep or permanent association with few is no longer viable, George Washington's warning against "entangling alliances" notwithstanding. As the gunslinging George W. Bush found in his war in Iraq, the United States had few allies willing to provide significant amounts of unconditional support. Nations in continental Europe, Asia, and the Middle East offered titular cooperation but little effective help. In 2003 Germany opposed the American role and France stood on the sidelines. To change this pattern, the United States needs to focus on primary allies to build unity, muscle, and economic strength. It must choose permanent associates and work with them, as it tried to do during the Cold War. Only in that way will America regain its former status as the major member of the strongest coalition in world politics.

The challenge of the East will be less worrisome to a tightly knit Western alliance. Although individual Eastern countries have grown, there is no Eastern unity. A Western combination of nations would constitute a sturdy rejoinder to Eastern gains. A more powerful West would also attract democratic members from the East, like Japan. It would be better equipped to deal with the worldwide challenges of recession and the constantly enlarging global marketplace. The region that gains the greatest size, bringing together the major centers of industrial and technological power, will have the advantage in setting the terms of development for years to come.[4] If China, India, and Asia remain at odds politically and territorially, the United States and European Union can create a new and profound association among themselves. Europe can meanwhile add new members to its economic and currency union, further enhancing its collective weight in world politics. The West's enlargement could compensate for its failure to develop at China's or India's pace.

If, on the other hand, the United States goes its own way, one rising nation after another will surpass it, bringing on the very challenges that in the past led to world war. American decline will change from a visible danger to a present reality. How can the West come together, and what roles may West and East play? These questions are the subject of this book.

# ONE

# The Size of States

The demand for economic and political size among states has changed over time, but not always in the same direction: the ideal size of a state has gone up and down and then up again. In the classical period from roughly 2000 B.C. to 1000 A.D., traditional monarchies and empires sought larger size. Five hundred years later, trading cities like Venice, Genoa, and then Amsterdam were content to be small so long as they could get spices, salt, and sugar from the East and West Indies. Then everything changed: first, large powers like France and Austria introduced gunpowder weapons, threatening the existence of smaller units; second, a mercantilist fascination with gold led countries like England to push exports and diminish imports, punishing those smaller entities like the Dutch, who favored open trade.

What influences size is the openness of international commerce. Large size wins out when international trade is restricted and, more recently, when capital flows dwarf the wealth of individual economies. As to the first, even a successful trading country may be forced to get larger if it no longer can export to markets overseas. Facing restrictions on its trade, it has to sell to its own population. Such countries need larger territories (with resources and people to match) to sustain their positions. Military factors may also make large territorial scale important, as offensive weapons begin to leap over fortifications or river barriers that previously protected small nations. Today, countries also seek larger size if they are undermined by sudden movements of capital out of their economies. Finally, if countries get larger, they are likely to gain a greater diversity of talents and factors of production, which likely translate into a greater variety of products and services. They may acquire key raw materials. Large countries may then get economies of scale in production.

In the contemporary world, economic size has become a primary need. In nominal terms, the international economy has grown by a factor of sixty in the past half century, from $1 trillion in 1960 to $61 trillion in 2010. Facing such massive wealth, countries need size to cope with the bigger scale of international factor movements and financial flows.[1]

In earlier centuries, the usual way for a nation to gain size was through conquest.[2] Julius Caesar, Napoleon Bonaparte, and British imperial proconsuls like Cecil Rhodes magnified their realm's power by taking over land, population, and resources from less organized regions. Rome extended its sway from Mesopotamia to the edge of Scotland; Napoleon administered a realm that included the Low Countries, the Rhineland, North Italy, Spain, and Austria. Britain assembled an empire that embraced one-fourth of the land area and one-seventh of the population of the globe. Medieval China and ancient Egypt also sought the economic and political benefits of territorial size.

A state could also achieve scale through inheritance or voluntary accession. France absorbed the duchy of Burgundy when the last duke died without an heir in 1477. It could not, however, keep his widely scattered territories together. On the whole, empires were built by force of arms. The United States of America grew in size by defeating British, French, Spanish, and Mexican opponents during the eighteenth and nineteenth centuries. Sometimes states gave way voluntarily rather than come into conflict with American expansion. France agreed to the Louisiana Purchase and Russia to the sale of Alaska as the inexorable westward movement of American pioneers encroached on their realms. Mexico fought America's drive to the Pacific but ended up surrendering half its lands to the ever enlarging nation.

Conquest could be expensive, but if it succeeded, the conqueror acquired new stores of grain, peasants, and a larger tax base to defray the cost of acquisition. Economic historians estimate that until 1815 or so, the use of force to gain territory easily repaid itself.[3] Britain ruled much of the world—civilized and uncivilized—for a veritable pittance. A millennium and a half earlier, Roman commanders had paraded their booty and captives through the streets of the capital to awe citizens and increase their own political sway. For hundreds of years, riches flowing to Rome paid for its military exertions. Forceful conquest was also the primary means by which the Austrian Empire, the Russian Empire, and Napoleonic France consolidated territory in Europe.[4]

In the sixteenth century Hernán Cortés invaded Mexico

and overawed much more numerous Aztec forces with horses and gunpowder, neither of which had they previously seen or heard. When Cortés charged on horseback and seized the emperor's banner, Mexican resistance collapsed. Cortés got silver and gold for his trouble, increasing the Spanish ruler's wealth and power.

The outcome of conquest also depended on the costs of war. If a leader conscripted too many grain-producing peasants into the army, he might cause a food shortage at home.[5] This happened to Russia during the First World War and helped bring on the Russian Revolution. But until quite recently, war was typically self-financing. If a king could seize specie (gold and silver), cochineal (red dye), and spices (everything from pepper to cloves) or Brazilian sugar cane, he could raise money to rule his kingdom and finance his armies. Sixteenth-century Spain paid for its military campaigns against Holland with gold and silver extracted from the mines of Peru and Mexico.[6] In the seventeenth and eighteenth centuries, Europeans financed their wars by trading for Eastern delicacies. At the end of the Seven Years' War (1756–63), William Pitt the Elder, who directed English military ventures, could claim that commerce had been made to flourish through war as England took Canada from France and got Florida and sugar islands in the bargain. Having seized Calcutta and most of India in 1758, Pitt and the British East India Company presided over an England that was quickly becoming the greatest imperial power on earth. The way to greatness was through conquest of territory.

Do countries need greater scale now? And should America favor aggressive expansion today? Certainly not. Nations do need greater size because the problems they confront are the kind that scale can remedy, but territorial aggression brings the worse problem of war. Nations today can amass size by other means, notably through the extension of customs unions and a kind of intermixture of sovereignty among their members. Nations are not organizing themselves into new sovereign states, but they are granting authority to larger entities.

In response to Russian increases in strength and territory after 1945, the United States and Europe formed the North Atlantic Treaty Organization, which placed the defense of Europe under a joint military command. The European nations have since 1999 pooled much of their economic sovereignty under a common currency, the euro. But these aggregations of power were never confederated into an all-embracing political or economic union.[7]

## Economic Size and Power

A large territory historically was not the only means to economic power. Long-distance commerce over open trading routes offered an alternative to geographical expansion. The contrast between Russia and Portugal illustrates this point. The Russian land mass extended from Europe to Asia but yielded meager returns to the tsar because Russia lacked a commercial economy and its peasants were poor. Tiny Portugal and later the Netherlands gained monopolies on trade with India and the East Indies in the sixteenth and seventeenth centuries. They earned great returns by selling Eastern specialties for high prices throughout Europe. Venice, Portugal, and Holland did not have to get bigger to prosper.[8]

Economic size can compensate for small territorial size. This legerdemain, however, is no longer possible for the contemporary United States. Economic growth, by itself, will not return America or the West to their past positions of grandeur. Foreign trade in today's restricted world will not rejuvenate their fortunes. The reason is that a nation can make the leap from underdeveloped to developed only one time. Once it creates a well-heeled middle class, economic growth declines; people already have most of what they need, and the nation's domestic market cannot grow at double-digit rates. Population growth declines. By then, furthermore, labor costs have caused manufacturers to shift some of their production elsewhere. In current economic and technological circumstances, Western sales abroad will never make up for rapid Eastern growth.[9]

## Major Shifts in Size

If the world were completely open and economic and trade flows were unlimited, greater national size would not be necessary. There would be a single world market and source of finance.[10] But because no single political and economic organization has ever been able to unite the entire world, national borders have always restricted trade and capital flows over much of the globe. This restriction has affected small and large political units differently. Big units with a wealth of population and raw materials have done better under conditions of closed-off markets; small units prospered when the world economy was more open.

*Homo sapiens* emerged as a recognizable species 150,000 years ago. Hunter-gatherers of the Mesolithic and Neolithic ages formed the smallest economic units. No social units larger than a small tribe could be formed out of households under these conditions. Not until about 10,000 B.C. did humans begin to cultivate crops and domesticate animals.

Since then, there have been three broad shifts in the size of economy and of territory. The first was a period of state closure or neglect of foreign trade. For roughly three thousand years, from about 2000 B.C. to 1000 A.D., the most successful economic entities were large agglomerations of power. In dry areas with one or two major river systems, despotisms in Egypt, China, and India monopolized water and irrigation and extracted loyalty from their dependent peasants.[11] In rainy areas like Europe and the Mediterranean, a more complex system developed. The Roman republics and then the Roman Empire offered protection to conquered provinces and facilitated trade along newly built Roman roads and waterways. Roman citizens prospered through contributions from vassal states. After defeating Carthage in the Punic Wars in 201 B.C., Roman power spread throughout the Mediterranean basin.[12]

At its height, Rome ruled an empire that extended from Hadrian's Wall (dividing England from Scotland) into Turkey, Mesopotamia, Egypt, and North Africa. From the Rhine to the Danube to the Tigris, Roman power determined security and welfare for its inhabitants. This did not mean that Rome directly administered this entire area. It was largely presided over by client states like Thrace, Palmyra, Cappadocia, and Arabia. Rome's informal suzerainty lasted for centuries, though it did not match China's record of millennial endurance.

On the fringes of the Roman enterprise, "barbarians" (Franks and Goths) picked away at vulnerable provinces. The cost of defending them made Rome's debt grow to huge proportions. Barbarian invasions from across the Rhine intruded into Roman territory. At home, individual military commanders vied for influence and power. By the fourth century of the Christian era, when Constantine gathered the reins of power into his own hands, Roman military legions had increased to between 200,000 and 300,000 men. The enhanced army augmented security for the Roman territories, but taxes to pay for it also rose. Rome granted citizenship to men living in outlying areas, and these new citizens refilled the armies, but Rome's lengthy frontiers, amounting to tens of thousands of miles, created huge military burdens that Rome ultimately could not support, despite tributes and exactions from subsidiaries. Still, although the Roman Empire experienced a precipitate decline after the third century A.D., there was no sudden collapse of political authority. In the fourth century, Constantine moved his headquarters to Byzantium on the Black Sea, while the Western marches of the previous empire dissolved into cities and their associated countrysides. Italy no longer presided over the world. But Rome bequeathed its influence to three other large institutions.

First, the Catholic Church emerged after 400 A.D. as a territorial power with growing influence. It controlled much of Italy and asserted influence over Western and German kings in the eighth century.[13] Second, German potentates set up the Holy Roman Empire—a political edifice centered around Austria to solidify their thrones against the pope. If the pope was to acquire temporal authority, the German kings would create new political states to resist him. Third, inspired by the Prophet Mohammed, Islamic invaders took over North Africa and much of Spain between 900 and 1000. They established Muslim control of the Holy Land until the Crusades challenged them and briefly reclaimed the formerly Christian areas after 1100. None of these political or religious agglomerations solved the problem of organizing legitimate rule over an accepting population that from time to time had to be consulted about its wishes. Ultimately these attempts at conquest and administration were far less successful than their Roman predecessor's.

The last territorial empire in medieval history was founded by Genghis Khan in the thirteenth century. During this period, nomadic horsemen traveled from Mongolia to Asia to create an empire six thousand miles across. But these nomadic rulers, with fifty thousand horsemen—in effect "roving bandits"— were less efficient or lasting than the "stationary bandits" represented by traditional kings. Military nomads pillaged their own conquered territories, making stable rule impossible.[14] The Mongol Empire endured for 150 years but gave way to rule by successor kings, sultans, or emperors who protected agriculture, the lifeblood of the realm. Free from foreign attack, land-bound populations gained the security to produce crops. During this period, large landed regimes emerged in post-Mongol China, in India, and in Egypt. These agricultural polities did not depend on foreign trade. Again the world saw the creation of large agglomerations of territorial power. The growth of these empires represented the first stage in the acquisition of size.

## Small Units

With navigational advances and longer range ships, trade beckoned in the thirteenth century, and with it another method of economic success became available. Long-distance trade allowed a country that was master of markets or particular technologies to become wealthy while remaining small. Venice was a classic example. An early proponent of trade with the East, it never sought territorial expansion but fashioned a trading network that brought food from the shores of the Black Sea and sent Venetian glass, textiles, and salt to Eastern ports.[15] Venice and later Genoa made more on trade in the thirteenth century than the much larger French monarchy received in taxes.[16]

When Portugal and Holland entered the world of trade between 1500 and 1600, they showed that a country could virtually subsist on commerce alone. These trading nations did not have to attack contemporaries or acquire land mass: all they needed was the ability to purchase exotic and valued commodities in Asia, which they could then sell in Europe at a premium price. They also required a potent naval force to convey the goods back to the West. While Lisbon and Amsterdam did need trading enclaves in India and the Eastern Antilles, they did not have to annex and run large political empires. Theirs was a dexterous trading network in which products, not people, were the subjects of interest. These small state units had established legitimacy within their own frontiers—landed estates and cities agreed to cooperate together to carry on imperial policy outside. What they could not do, however, was to solve the problem of imperial organization—how to organize a vast empire that treated the periphery differently from the center.[17] This inequality created a grievance that led colonies to revolt against their masters from the eighteenth through the twentieth centuries.

Small countries striving to run great empires also faced difficulties at home. By 1500, the spread of gunpowder, which gave birth to siege guns and naval men of war, began to threaten the smaller states' independence. One by one, their autonomy at home was undermined by military siege or naval blockade, and larger states came to replace or absorb them. The coming of the Industrial Revolution enhanced this trend. In the eighteenth century, coal-fueled machine production of woolen and then cotton cloth gave British mills an advantage over all competitors, including the Dutch. Their superiority came from technology, not trade in exotic goods. Countries with coal or other energy sources capitalized on sudden advantages. Economic and territorial size, however, did not immediately increase. Britain exported textiles and railway equipment throughout the world, and this new production multiplied English national income. In the 1840s, British foreign trade (exports and imports) was about 40 percent of GDP, about the same as China's today. Other countries, like Germany and Russia, had to catch up to develop at similar rates. Germany began to export chemicals and pharmaceuticals, and Russia sent huge grain shipments from Odessa to Western ports. By the end of the century, Central and Eastern European powers matched and even exceeded British rates of development. The United States also harnessed its agriculture and exported food and raw materials to many other countries. In the twentieth century, the further progress of industrialization allowed the United States to ship autos, electrical goods, and then petroleum to many other nations. But territorial size was not the country's great advantage. As long as trade barriers were low, countries did not yet have to get larger.

## Imperial Size

Still, imperial size had been growing for centuries. Britain acquired India in the mid–eighteenth century and much of Africa by the third quarter of the nineteenth century. France took West Africa, and Germany part of East Africa. What the Great Powers could not agree to divide among themselves they left to Portugal, Holland, and Belgium.

The demand for size quickened in the last quarter of the

nineteenth century. When European countries and America raised tariffs during the Great Depression of 1873–96, nations could no longer rely on trade to augment their growth. Leaders of depressed economies, fearing that imports from other countries would undermine their industries at home, put on restrictions to prevent it. Germany, Austria, and Russia moved to protect their food and iron industries. The United States raised tariffs on foreign manufactured goods. France added higher tariffs in 1893. Only England stayed faithful to free trade, suffering partial exclusion from European markets, and relying instead on the British Empire. Its rate of development, which had been based on foreign trade, further declined.

The rise of tariff barriers brought the age of imperialism to its apex. As long as the international economy was open, states could sell in foreign markets without demanding territorial control. But when the trading system closed down at the end of the nineteenth century, it became necessary to become territorially "big." If Britain could not sell effectively in Europe and America, it needed colonies overseas that would take its goods. British imperial expansion after 1880 was marked by the practice, articulated by the foreign secretary, Lord Rosebury, of "pegging out [colonial] claims for the future" that would offer markets and raw materials to London when European markets closed. Imperial access to Asia and Africa became the remedy for shrinking international openness. By 1938 tropical Africa represented nearly 60 percent of Britain's southern hemisphere colonies, compared with only 2 percent before 1880.[18]

Britain had vital sales in its empire—to India, Australia, Canada, and South Africa. Germany and Japan possessed smaller markets abroad and only tiny empires: they had to sell at home or to regional markets nearby. These countries became late expansionists.[19] South Asia, Africa, and then the Balkans (formerly the property of the Ottoman Empire) were divided up among imperial claimants like Austria, which annexed Bosnia, and Russia, which had an effective protectorate over Bulgaria and was closely linked to Serbia. Rumania was independent but aligned with Germany.

The number of states in the world system declined as England, France, Russia, and the United States took more territories. The United States got Puerto Rico and the Philippines as a result of its war with Spain in 1898.

This imperialism did not last. In the 1950s, Western rule in Africa provoked nationalist revolutions resulting in the creation of postcolonial nations like Ghana, Kenya, and Tanzania. The world now has more than two hundred states. In the 1970s and 1980s the United States was thrown out of Vietnam, and Russia was ejected from Afghanistan. The breakup of the Russian Empire added fourteen new states to the international system. The United States itself is now in the course of withdrawing from "nation-building" experiments in Iraq and Afghanistan.

In the 1970s and 1980s, commercial countries like Japan, West Germany, and the Asian tigers attained international prominence as they grew faster than giants like the Soviet Union and the United States. These small trading states did not have territorial ambitions or try to project military power abroad. While the United States was entangled in Vietnam and the Soviet Union in Afghanistan, trading states concentrated on gaining economic access to foreign territories rather than political control. For a time they were successful.

The trading state model, however, ran into unexpected problems in the 1990s. Japanese growth stalled after 1987 when interest rates rose, crushing the linked equity and housing markets. In contrast, American productivity and growth surged forward. Many trading states were rocked by the Asian financial crisis of 1997–98, in which the sudden withdrawal of money by foreign investors caused a sharp reversal of capital flows, with the departure of $50 billion of private capital. Investors feared that Thailand and Indonesia could not pay their bills and acted accordingly. Then the crisis spread to Malaysia and South Korea. Debt rating agencies downgraded Far Eastern countries, causing a further run on East Asian banks. In 1998 Malaysia contracted by 7.5 percent, Korea by 6.7 percent, Thailand by 10.4 percent, and Indonesia by 13.2 percent. As foreigners removed their monies, these countries did not have enough capital to withstand the shock. As Alan Greenspan, then chairman of the U.S. Federal Reserve, put it: "They had no spare tires." To restore momentum, governments devalued their zcurrencies and adopted high interest rates, but they did not regain their former growth. The process was two-fold: first speculators took out their funds; then international agencies required devaluation and contraction to bail out the debtor nations.

Russia also fell afoul of creditors. With the oil price falling, Moscow could not service its loans in 1998 and defaulted on its government bonds. Russia's problem was that although its territory was vast, its economy—based on oil and natural gas—was too small to cover its ambitious commitments in infrastructure and higher growth. China and India, on the other hand, had plenty of access to cash, and their economies remained on a steady upward course.

Small trading states failed because the assumptions on which they operated did not hold. To succeed, they needed an open international market into which they could sell easily and from which they could borrow quickly. But in 1997 and 1998, the markets of the developed world were not sufficiently open to absorb the trading states' goods. These states could not redeem themselves through quick sales abroad, nor could they borrow on easy terms.[20] Instead, they had to kneel at the altar of international finance and accept dictation from the International Monetary Fund, whose financial assistance came with onerous conditions (including devaluation and higher interest rates) attached. Low growth and higher unemployment were the result.

Some might hypothesize that this outcome represents a "requiem" for the trading state in the twenty-first century. This is not true, although the prospect for small trading states has dimmed. Instead of accepting openness and small size, developing nations have sought larger size and increasingly opted for mercantilism, tariffs, subsidies, and state-sponsored industry to meet economic challenges. Developing states have sought greater territorial access to raw materials, capital, and trained labor supplies, with manufacturing increasingly based at home. This does not mean, however, that "conquest" outmodes "commerce" as the modus operandi of international politics. The "trading state" of the 1980s and 1990s gave up "conquest" as a vain undertaking. The "large state" of today agrees, but it has sought economic enlargement through customs union and preferential tariff arrangements with key markets and suppliers to gain greater economic size and the growth that hopefully goes with it.

In the aftermath of the 1997–98 crisis, small trading states vowed never to put themselves in a similar position, and they increased their access to foreign exchange through exports. Korea, Thailand, Indonesia, and others built up larger reserves of foreign currency. They proposed a regional trade arrangement with a preferential tariff zone in which to sell their goods.

## The Growth of Global Markets

The need for size has been accentuated by the exponential growth of global markets. The *New York Times* calculated (using Bank of International Settlements data) that derivatives contracts—financial instruments tied to existing indices—totaled $600 trillion in 2010,[21] ten times world GDP. These contracts were continuing to rise in value. As banks and hedge funds wrote derivatives contracts to cover potential losses, the amount of money at risk rose with them. When Greece looked insolvent, hedge funds bought its bonds at bargain-basement prices, hoping that they would ultimately recoup large amounts when the bonds came due. In more general terms, as investors take a negative position on individual countries—shorting the countries' assets—they can force any cash-poor borrower to its knees, as happened to Thailand and Indonesia in 1997. Investors took similarly negative positions against Greece and Portugal after 2010; such investors only failed because the European Central Bank and the IMF (along with Germany and France) came to Greece and Portugal's rescue. All of these episodes underscore one vital point: unless a country has access to huge amounts of cash, it can be vulnerable to well-heeled speculators who can borrow funds on a leveraged basis from largely unregulated banks.

Money coming into a country can be an unexpected and sometimes unwanted boon (because of its inflationary effects); money leaving can spell disaster. Local inflation and deflation can result from the actions of untutored but powerful investors far from the scene. Even the United States would suffer if funds rushed to other international locations, as they threatened to do in the global crisis of 2008–9.

While stock markets were losing 50 percent of their value in 2008 and 2009, U.S. interest rates remained low because capital did not leave: China, Japan, and Europe continued to buy and hold large amounts of American government securities. Had foreign investors removed their funds, U.S. interest rates would have shot up as they did in 1979. In 1978 and again in 1979, there was a run on the dollar as inflation rose above interest rates. Fed chairman Paul Volcker then hiked interest rates and levied contraction on the economy as a result: de facto the United States had to accept a recession to restore its position. The lesson is that even the biggest players were too small to surmount such a crisis on their own.

## Free Trade Versus the Need for Territory

History reveals an inverse relationship between free trade and the advantages for a nation of holding large amounts of territory. Large empires tended to emerge during the long periods when the world economy was partly or mostly closed. When nations eased economic barriers and welcomed trade, states could be small as long as they had navies to carry specialty goods from exotic locations back to Europe. Another factor that presaged increasing difficulty later over time for the small state, however, was the introduction of gunpowder into European battles.[22] When the Industrial Revolution occurred to offer new and cheaper goods, trade rose again, but it could not survive the restricting effect of tariffs in the late nineteenth century. Once more, states chose territorial expansion to create large empires. During the Cold War large agglomerations of power dominated, but small trading states challenged them in the 1960s to 1980s. Decolonization in Africa led to new regional organizations. These were supplemented by larger groupings of power like the European Union and the North Atlantic Free Trade Area as tariffs and economic restrictions returned once more.

Today, territorial expansion through conquest does not succeed; instead nations achieve large-scale production through the creation of new customs unions like NAFTA, Mercosur, and the East African Customs Union. More than a hundred preferential trade arrangements have been created in the past generation. It has become necessary to increase the size of economic units because no single nation, however large, can cope with the challenges it confronts.

# TWO

# The Rise of the East

History records continual transfers of economic and political power from one region to another. In any period, the dominant economic core has always needed the labor force and resources of the periphery to remain strong—just as the West needs the labor force of East Asia to produce its goods today. In the past, economic primacy alternated between core and periphery.

Assisting and then ultimately vying with Spain between 1580 and 1640, the small states of Portugal and then Holland rose to become the core of the international economic system. But that power was not long retained. Dutch power gave way to that of Great Britain, Austrian power to France, and French power to Britain. America was originally the periphery for Great Britain, but it ultimately replaced Britain as the core of the world economic system. This chapter seeks to show that the East has risen, but it is not a united entity today, nor is it likely to become one. The East has established no single core, and the rising peripheries are associated with the West as closely as with other members of the East.

In the twentieth century, international economists argued that capital and labor would move to the regions in which development lagged.[1] A country with cheaper labor and greater availability of land would attract overseas investment, and the backward economy would gradually grow to equalize its position with the more developed world. Because its labor and other costs were less, goods produced in the backward economy would have a relative price advantage over those made in advanced countries. What is surprising is that the growth of the developing countries has taken so long. Agricultural countries in Africa and Latin America have remained behind in their development.

This was not always the case. In the third quarter of the nineteenth century, the United States, Russia, Australia, Canada, and South Africa were all emerging economies. They specialized in agricultural commodities and raw materials and readily exported their goods to Europe, receiving a solid return and usually an export surplus in the bargain. Their standards of living rose, greatly facilitated by a decline in transport costs and the availability of refrigeration for their perishable food exports.

When tariffs rose after World War I, a new set of emergent nations—now in Latin America, Asia, and Africa—could no longer easily export their wares to more advanced countries, and their markets stagnated. Instead of possessing a terms-of-trade advantage in which food and raw materials were highly or at least fairly valued, African and Latin American commodity prices fell compared with Western industrial goods. Inflation and production shortages deriving from slow reconversion after World War II made European and American industrial products even more expensive. At the same time, Western countries put tariffs on agricultural goods and strove to become more self-sufficient in food production, leaving less advantaged nations with little to offer. Industrial trade between Europe and the United States replaced the old exchange of food for manufactures between advanced and developing regions of the world.[2]

Unable to sell their agricultural products, third-world producers tried to compete in industry but were not initially successful. Early versions of Indian and Brazilian cars, tractors, and airplanes were not sufficiently advanced or well-made to attract Western markets. (The Yugo—an automobile made in Serbia and introduced to the U.S. market in 1979—is a well-known example.) Developing countries sustained these nascent industries by putting tariffs on industrial products, striving to keep their home markets for their own products. But the strategy of import-substituting industrialization only led to shoddy and inefficient goods.[3] Unlike their nineteenth-century American predecessors, they had no cornucopia of new inventions to rely on.

The oil crises of 1973 and 1979 opened a new era. The Middle Eastern oil producers had earned huge amounts on their petroleum exports but did not spend the proceeds. They kept their cash in Western bank accounts and demanded a high return. Western banks in turn lent this money to the developing countries, which readily took the cash. But the recession of 1982 undermined their markets abroad and led developing country borrowers to default on their bank loans, which then had to be refinanced. The lenders took large losses.

# The Rise of the East

By the mid-1980s, capital was once again flowing to Eastern countries in large and regular amounts. Western producers of televisions, electronics, and industrial equipment found cheaper component manufacturers in Asia and Latin America. Mexico, Korea, Indonesia, Malaysia, and Thailand turned out Western goods in quantity. For the first time, offshore production chains were set up to make original equipment manufacturers more efficient. Production of intermediate components and final assembly could be devolved to Asians, particularly to China, which had a large skilled workforce and low labor costs. The Asian task then became to move to higher links in the production chain, producing at successively more sophisticated rungs in the manufacturing ladder. Asians had done assembly and component production, but they wanted to move closer to the design of the product. This did not occur right away, and Asian proceeds from foreign trade, though substantial, remain constrained even today. Self-sufficient Asian development was a long time in coming.

China was economically almost inert under Mao, and Russia was stagnant under Stalin and his successors. In the 1950s, India was in the throes of Nehru's anti-capitalist rhetoric and the state controlled most economic activity above the level of subsistence agriculture. Import substitution greatly slowed economic development. The protected Russian manufacturing industry was incredibly inefficient, as were those in Latin America and South Asia. The Lada—a Russian-made car based on a 1955 Fiat—plied Soviet and later Egyptian roads for decades, but it was never much improved.

Not until key Asian states like Japan, Singapore, Hong Kong, and Korea began to export abroad did economic resurgence occur. These smaller countries set themselves to compete in the toughest markets, Europe and the United States, recognizing that they might fail. Mostly, Asians became component manufacturers, though Japan decided on a frontal assault across the industrial board—in cars, televisions, electronics, machinery, and pianos. (Nissan Motors for a time masqueraded as "Datsun" in North America because it did not want the Nissan name attached if its cars did not succeed.)[4] Japanese companies drew domestic U.S. support because they combined Japanese design, engineering, and lower costs with assembly plants in Kentucky, Ohio, and Tennessee. Workers in these plants generally were not unionized, so labor costs could be kept down. Meanwhile, General Motors, Ford, and Chrysler were not admitted to markets in Japan and were unable, at first, to set up production in Asia.

The product life cycle hypothesis of Raymond Vernon helped to explain the sequence of production decisions.[5] A Harvard Business School professor, Vernon cited the example of television sets, but it applied to computers as well. To begin with, American innovators produced television sets for the home market and then exported abroad; they first sent television sets to Europe and Japan in the 1960s. In a second stage, competitors in Europe and Japan sought to capture their own markets. Later, as they became more efficient, Europe and China sought to export cheaper sets to the United States. In a final stage, Europe, Japan, and the United States all had their sets produced in developing countries overseas (Mexico, Korea, China, Taiwan, or Thailand) for import to the home country.

As these new industries developed abroad, higher-cost U.S. plants were increasingly outpaced. All television sets are now assembled elsewhere, and the same is true of computers. American labor has opposed "outsourcing," believing that American industries—based on high-cost labor—cannot compete. But this does not mean that design, engineering, financing, and marketing will necessarily devolve to others. In fact, the processes that contribute the most value added to the product are in the higher stages of the production chain. If the United States designs the product and retains high-end manufacturing at home, outsourcing the lower or final stages to other countries adds to American competitiveness and improves Western standards of living. The United States, Canada, and Finland produce cell-phones abroad (in Vietnam, Thailand, or China), but they still capture the lion's share of the monetary and technical benefits from computer chips, marketing, and design from the ultimate sales of goods.[6]

The rise of the East has taken time. As we have seen, agriculture did not provide a solution to developing the Third World of the 1950s—Africa, Latin America, and rice-rich areas of East Asia. It was not until Korea proved that it could prosper from manufacturing that the developing world tilted away from farming and in favor of industry. In 1959 South Korea was an agricultural nation with a GDP of three hundred dollars per capita. After it started manufacturing chips for Western computers, it quickly became an industrial and exporting powerhouse that excelled in specialty after specialty: DRAM chips, automobiles, flat panel screens, chemicals, and appliances of all kinds. Korea also availed itself of industrial ties to Japan, incorporating Japanese components into its products. By the 1980s Korean dexterity and inventiveness had so impressed the hidebound Soviet Union that Mikhail

Gorbachev hoped that Russia could follow a similar tack. It turned out that it could not, and Russia had to rely instead on oil and natural gas to power its economy.

## The Rise of China

China's rise awaited the leadership of Deng Xiaoping in 1978.[7] Mao's backyard steel mills and the so-called "great leap forward" only delayed development.[8] The Cultural Revolution decimated university education by directing students into the countryside to do menial jobs. Only when Deng concluded that foreign trade could lead China's growth did matters begin to change. Taking a leaf from the successful Japanese and German industrializations in the nineteenth century, Deng gradually opened the country up, focusing first on "special economic zones" like Guangdong, Fujian, and Dalian, where joint ventures with foreign capital were permitted. Large amounts of foreign direct investment came into those zones, and cheap labor costs allowed China to assemble Western and Japanese goods for later shipment abroad. This was the final stage of Ray Vernon's product life cycle. As the returns came in, China invested more and more in such ventures and output spurted ahead, moving beyond special economic zones and out into the countryside.

For a time it appeared that China's growth was simply the result of more "inputs" leading to greater output, with no productivity gains involved.[9] In the 1990s there was little productivity growth. Later, however, China was able to improve its return per unit of input, and it has continued doing so. Therefore China no longer needs investment rates of 40 percent of GDP to keep growing; 20 or 30 percent would be consistent with high growth sustained increasingly by productivity improvement. According to China Development Research Foundation economists, total factor productivity has risen between 1 and 2 percent each year since 1997.[10] This increase still does not mean that China has caught or will catch up to the United States or even France in overall productivity.[11]

Of greater long-term importance is the stability of the Chinese Communist regime. The rise of the middle class, which in 2015 will constitute about 30 percent of the population, or 400 million individuals, would normally involve changes in governance.[12] In country after country in East Asia and Latin America, the rise of the middle class has led to the installation of democracy.[13] Brazil, Indonesia, South Korea, Colombia, Mexico, Malaysia, Taiwan, and the Philippines are only a few examples of developing countries that became legitimate democracies when their incomes rose. This has not happened in China, though the regime tries to pay attention to public opinion through repeated polling of its citizens. More than one hundred thousand instances of political or economic resistance to government action still take place every year in China. People do not like their property being seized to build new dams or railways and resent the stingy "eminent domain" payments they receive for agreeing to these ventures. Where earthquakes have shown inadequate building standards, people denounce authorities and demand change, as they did in Sichuan province after the earthquake in 2008. There are resistance movements in Tibet and Xinjiang (where the Uighur population resides) and where people are culturally and linguistically different from the dominant Han population of China. The CCP still lacks democratic legitimacy.

It is true that the government holds elections (among Communist candidates) at the village level. But if the regime does not expand elections beyond the village level, benefiting from that democratization, it may have to manufacture a resurgence of nationalism to keep the population in line and itself in power. China's rapid recovery from the economic crisis of 2008–9 mitigated discontent, but it will rise again when foreign threats appear. I was in Beijing in April 2005 at a time of economic prosperity, when the visits of Japanese prime minister Junichiro Koizumi to the Yasukuni Shrine in Tokyo, where Japanese war criminals are interred, led to spontaneous and possibly also government-supported attacks on Japanese consulates in China. Windows were broken and doorways smashed. The riots continued for two weeks before the government and protestors subsided. Such displays will unquestionably return, whether triggered by the regime or not.

China poses a very interesting example of the limits of economic interest in charting the long-term policy of a partly authoritarian government. No country is today more dependent on the relative openness of the international economy than China. It is totally dependent on the U.S. Navy to secure the sea lanes to the Middle East and provide access to desperately needed oil. China's development has been tied to sales of its goods in Japan, Europe, and the United States because the domestic market—still not that of a fully middle-class nation—cannot absorb these manufactures. Unlike Germany or Japan in 1890 or 1920, China's further growth does not depend on finding new markets. It already has those markets, as well as plenty of access to all the raw materials it needs. It has special relationships with African countries, Brazil, and Australia to source key minerals and other resources. It has access to the oil of the Middle East. In short, no rising Great Power has been so fully a beneficiary of the existing state of affairs as China.

And yet China's acceptance of that system, given its incomplete democracy, remains in question.

## The Rise of India

India's course has been completely different. It never had a Deng Xiaoping to force development into a new and more successful path. Jawaharlal Nehru once noted that India was like "some ancient palimpsest on which layer upon layer of thought and reverie had been inscribed and yet no succeeding layer had completely hidden or erased what had been written previously."[14] India always absorbed goods, ideas, and people from outside. As late as 1700 it produced a quarter of world GDP, according to the economic historian Angus Maddison. India then had a self-sufficient economy, and trade in Indian textiles, for example, had to be paid for by gold from mines in Central and South America. Indeed India became known as "the sink" for such rare metals.

In the aftermath of independence from the British Raj in 1947, India had to overcome the economic ideas of its founders: Mahatma (Mohandas K.) Gandhi and Jawaharlal Nehru. Having imported British industrial goods and Lancashire cottons for many years, Gandhi wished to return the country to homespun industries and declare independence from industrialism. Nehru, however, believed in state-run industries, which almost completely cut out the private sector. It was not until 1991, under Prime Minister P. V. Narasimha Rao and Finance Minister Manmohan Singh, that the process of liberalizing the economy began to take place. Under the next prime minister, Atal Bihari Vajpayee, the Bharatiya Janata Party (BJP) focused on high-tech services and back-office functions in Bangalore and elsewhere. But it was not until Singh became prime minister, in 2004, that the process really accelerated. Most of the Indian National Congress governments before that time were composed of Nehru-style statists who distrusted the private sector and sought narrowly to control and direct economic growth, thinking always of its effects on poor peasants and the traditional rural social structure. Because of excessive government regulations, those days have been referred to as the "Permit-License Quota Raj." But the Congress government of Dr. Singh (supervised by Sonia Gandhi) has broadened its development effort to bring in new industrial as well as back-office projects.

When Singh became finance minister in 1991, Indian tariffs on manufactured goods were high and exports were minimal. But gradually, the success of high-tech services broadened into manufacturing, and now Tata Motors produces the Nano, the world's cheapest small car, which surprisingly is not selling well in India.[15] That does not mean, however, that Indians prefer foreign cars. It remains very difficult to export goods to India, and though the government set up Chinese-style special economic zones with greater freedom to innovate and associate with foreign companies, manufacturing remains a small fraction of GDP (less than 20 percent, while services are at about 50 percent of GDP).

Indian government regulations and bureaucratic inefficiency damp down this share. Indian courts enforce awards for breach of contract only after years of expensive litigation. Permission to set up companies or to import takes time. Indian tariffs are twice those in China. Foreign investors have hesitated to go into India because the infrastructure (roads, communications, and railways) is in poor condition. There are few rapid connections with ports, for example. Indian electric power is unreliable, with parts of the country blacked out during the day. Investors usually have to bring in their own power equipment if they want to manufacture there. Finally, there is a Communist rebellion in the south that pits the Maoist insurgents known as Naxalites against the regime. Fearing to sow discontent, ministers have been hesitant to allow big projects to proceed that might disrupt customary Indian life. India's democracy is very tradition-bound, and change comes excruciatingly slowly. Recently the government liberated retail trade, initially permitting Walmart to operate throughout India, but then it rescinded its reform, leaving economic uncertainty in its wake.

At the same time, India is making measurable progress. Yearly GDP growth is now at 7 percent, and even though India's population is still rising, there has been a noticeable increase in per capita GDP. The extension of television into the villages has given many Indians an understanding of how the rest of the world lives and what is ultimately possible for India as well. Rural education is poor, but the best Indian universities and technological centers are as good as MIT and Harvard. Hosts of new specialists and engineers are being trained, and they will continue opening India up to the effects of globalization. Indians are also aware of the challenge of China and are not hesitant to burnish their nationalist zeal in response. Similarly to China, however, India's neighbors are almost all hostile to Indian ambitions. Pakistan, Nepal, China, Bangladesh, and Sri Lanka are not supporters of Indian growth or its status as a great power. Only the United States has come in to redress the balance and support Indian development, even though India has not signed the Nuclear Non-Proliferation Treaty.

India sees itself as a rival to China and is extremely eager to keep up with or even surpass China's rise to power. With a more youthful population than its rival, India's growth rates may remain high for a longer period than China's. Per capita GDP in India, however, is one-third that of China, so it will take some years to catch up. Nonetheless, Angus Maddison calculates that by 2030, China will possess 23 percent, the United States 17 percent, and India 10 percent of world gross domestic product.[16]

## Other Players

Japan, Korea, Vietnam, and Singapore have also grown rapidly in the past twenty years. Japan attained its greatest development in the 1960s, tailing off to 4 percent in the 1980s and then 2 percent in the 2000s. South Korea rose in the 1970s when it manufactured items for Japan and later for other countries. It became a powerhouse in computer chips, cell phones, and auto manufacturing, ultimately challenging the Japanese domination of the American market. Vietnam is a new textile powerhouse, gaining market share from Hong Kong, China, Bangladesh, and Europe. It does low-labor-cost manufacturing, however, not advanced or technical innovation. Singapore has become a financial dynamo, distributing capital to willing recipients throughout Southeast Asia.

Each of these four countries is historically a rival of China, Japan most obviously so. Taro Aso, the Japanese foreign minister under both Junichiro Koizumi and Shinzo Abe, told a journalist in a somewhat unguarded moment: "Japan and China have hated each other for a thousand years. Why should things be any different now?"[17] South Korea, however, sought to diversify its reliance upon Japan by welcoming Chinese capital and markets. This did not mean that territorial or political issues were solved. Vietnam has detested China for centuries, dating back to its incorporation in the old Chinese Empire.

## Eastern Flying Geese

Taken over decades, the rise of the East has been staggering. But it is a rise of individual countries, not of an aggregated Eastern bloc. It fundamentally derived from Japan's economic success. Following in Japan's wake, like a formation of geese, other Eastern nations realized that they too could take a share of the industrial process and become links in overseas production chains. Japan assisted this shift by diversifying its own assembly to Korean, Thai, and Singaporean locations. This lessened the Japanese trade surplus with America, since the final stages of production were performed elsewhere. Many countries benefited from this rerouting of the Japanese surplus. Now, however, most products designed for the U.S. market have their final stage in China, the cheapest and most efficient of the East Asian producers. In this way, through linked outsourcing, many East Asian nations have gone up the economic ladder together. East Asia has been developing at 5–7 percent per year, while the United States and Europe grow at only 2–3 percent.

## South Korea, Taiwan, and Singapore

South Korea is in many ways the most efficient and forward-looking Asian producer; it started from scratch as an agricultural nation and has now become a vibrant industrial one, a new member of the Organization for Economic Cooperation and Development. Under a succession of authoritarian rulers from Syngman Rhee to Park Chung Hee, South Korea suffered military rule, initially caused by the postwar partition of the country, until the 1980s. With Park Chung Hee after 1962, however, it blossomed as a rapidly developing country with investments in cars, semiconductors, and electrical appliances of all types. General Park was in a sense the Deng Xiaoping of Seoul. Rather than promoting purely domestic industries, Park opted to create Korean industrial exports in partnership with private industry and partly in conjunction with Japanese multinational corporations. Progress was rapid until 1997–98, when *chaebol*—Korean family companies—over-borrowed from foreigners and briefly became insolvent, causing a quick recession. By the 2000s, however, Korea had resumed its upward track.

Developments after 1962 were different from what came before. Korea had initially aimed merely at import replacement, not to create firms that could compete on an international basis. By the 1980s, however, Korean enterprises in semiconductors, appliances, electronic equipment, cars, shipbuilding, and power generation had begun to compete effectively worldwide. Producing refrigerators, freezers, stoves, and air conditioners, LG may turn out to be the most efficient maker of white goods in the world. Hyundai will compete with Volkswagen and Toyota for leadership in cars. In addition to fully integrated consumer products, Korean companies also produced components for others. Samsung offered microchips for other companies' computers and telephones as well as televisions and electronic devices of its own. Yet unlike Taiwan, which (except for Acer) almost entirely manufactured components, flat screens, and software to be inserted into other countries' advanced products, Korea wanted name brands of its own. LG, Hyundai, and Samsung are the chief result. The country invested heavily—as much as 2 percent of

GDP—in research and development to keep up with Western and Japanese giants. Now Korea boasts the world's fastest computer. Although private industry has largely dictated the Korean course in recent years, its early phase of combined public and private efforts shows the long-term effectiveness of a joint strategy.

Taiwan is a different story. Its industrial development was started by Japan when it ruled Taiwan before 1945. Taiwanese components were designed to go into Japanese assembly of finished products. When Taiwan became independent of Japan, this industrial pattern continued. After achieving land reform, which liberated the rural population, Taiwan acquired a new labor force to work in the cities. Unlike Korea, Taiwan did not aim to create economy-of-scale industries that would operate across the board and sell in all markets. Instead it took a less dramatic position, setting up "fabs"—companies that had no proprietary product of their own but were designed to manufacture the products of outside firms. In semiconductors, TSMC took the designs of U.S., Japanese, and other firms and turned out products to order. American, Japanese, and German companies could become "virtual" (without productive capacity at home) because they could get Taiwan to manufacture to their specification. Acer, now competing to be the number-one computer firm in the world, is a notable exception. In other fields, Taiwan has served as a technical and manufacturing asset for mainland China. Increasingly, Taiwanese companies like Hon Hai (denominated as Foxconn in the West) migrate across the Taiwan Strait and do their production in the seacoast provinces of China. More than one million Taiwanese now live on the mainland, a number that may well increase. Most of these firms are developing intermediate components that can be finally assembled in China for export abroad. They will not have Taiwanese names on them. Partly as a result of this economic integration, Taiwanese political support for an accommodation with China has grown in recent years. Particularly in the major port city of Kaohsiung, however, there is still pressure for democratic change in China as a prelude to reunification. China will have to be much more imaginative than it has been of late to adjust to this pressure, and it will have to recruit stalwarts from the Kuomintang, the anti-communist ruling party of Taiwan, to advise China and assume positions of responsibility in Beijing. Long-term authoritarianism will not suffice.

Singapore raises still different questions. Lee Kwan Yew, the prime minister from 1959 to 1990, developed an economically liberal regime under authoritarian control in domestic politics. His People's Action Party has defeated all comers over the past forty years, combining electoral effectiveness with lawsuits directed against opposing politicians. Informally known as "Harry" Lee, he created the modern Republic of Singapore almost single-handedly. A Hakka Singaporean, Lee earned a double first at Cambridge and looked around for countries sufficiently challenging to warrant the application of his talents. He might have competed to rule the entire Federation of Malaysia (which Singapore briefly joined in 1963), a Malay-dominated nation with Chinese and Indian populations as well. Singapore's People's Action Party, led by Lee, is fundamentally Chinese-oriented; it might have attracted Chinese votes in Malaysia and undermined Malay control, though Lee himself did not learn Chinese until he was thirty-two years old. When the leaders of Malaysia's ruling United Malay National Organization (UMNO) understood this, they forced

Singapore, the base of Lee's political power, to secede and become an independent state in 1965. Elected prime minister of the new city-state, Lee succeeded in creating a delicate equipoise among Singapore's different ethnic groups, where Chinese were in the majority over Malays and Indians. His "managed democracy" allowed the PAP to win election after election. The government knew how people voted and apportioned rewards accordingly. Candidates from other parties could be sued, or otherwise intimidated. Lee's son, Lee Hsien Loong, was ultimately his father's successor as prime minister.

Under British rule, Singapore had always been an entrepôt (free port) and transshipment point for goods arriving from the Dutch East Indies and Malaya. The British acquired it in 1819 and ruled until 1957. British Singapore did not engage in manufacturing, but it did tether together the commodity trade of nations using the Straits of Malacca. After 1965, Singapore decided to manufacture components into finished products and opened itself to Western and Japanese investment to set up local firms for this purpose. To do this, Singapore needed a capital market, and Lee quickly created one, seeking to compete with Zurich as a financial center. Temasek, the sovereign wealth fund of Singapore—funded by the nation's high savings rate—scoured the world for investment opportunities and invested in developed and developing country markets. With outstanding hotels, Singapore's tourist industry attracted visitors from China, Japan, and Korea. Lee's rule was benign but it strictly regulated public behavior. Spitting on the sidewalk, for instance, was punishable by caning—ten or twenty blows of the stick for miscreant offenders. Petty crime rates fell in response. Government servants were paid liberally to forestall corruption. Overall, Singapore mediated between bigger powers, fashioning cooperation and making no waves. American, European, and Japanese investment ensured its success. Singapore became a kind of hard-nosed Switzerland.

## East Asian Tension

There is a vast difference between East Asia and Europe. Despite its belligerent past, Europe is today a coherent region; Asia is a region of feuding parties. In the 1950s, to resist communist pressure, the United States sought to get East Asians to join a Pacific pact similar to the Atlantic pact. But local rivalries made such an alliance impossible to achieve. Smaller arrangements had to be devised, such as the South East Asia Treaty Organization, or Manila Pact (which brought Thailand, the Philippines, Australia, New Zealand, and Pakistan together with the United States, France, and the United Kingdom in 1955), although it did not last very long. The neutralist countries, India and Indonesia, did not join, nor did Burma. The United States signed separate pacts with Japan and Korea, but these could not be worked into an overall arrangement. The initial attempts at alliances, largely directed against the Soviet Union, foundered on the resistance of many Asian nations to join with the United States after the Korean War. Asian neutralists felt they would do better letting the two blocs compete for their favor. Later, the rise of China changed attitudes, but not the willingness to join a region-wide pact. For a time the United States and such allies as Canada and Australia sought a Pacific-wide approach that would bring China into a group with them, but they were not successful. Despite partial groupings such as APEC, ASEAN, and ASEAN Plus Three, no overall arrangement could be reached to bridge the gap or bring all Far Eastern states together.[18] China and Japan each wanted their own economic customs or currency union that would exclude the other. China wanted to keep the United States out of an intensive free trade zone in East Asia. Australia and New Zealand were considered too European to get into a high-level Asian directorate.

But these hesitations were no greater than those barring a purely East Asian regionalism from emerging. Vietnam is as strongly anti-Chinese as Japan. South Korea is close to China economically but is reserved because of China's support for North Korea. Seoul was particularly upset by North Korean attacks on the *Cheonan*, a South Korean warship, and on Yeonpyong Island, where innocent South Korean campers were injured. China did nothing to reprimand Pyongyang in either case. Thailand, Indonesia, the Philippines, and Malaysia are additionally sensitive to the Chinese minorities living inside their borders. Though small in size, those communities have great economic clout, and they pay a great deal of attention to Beijing. The role of the "overseas Chinese" financially and politically in Southeast Asia furthers Chinese influence and perhaps pressure.

Chinese territorial ambitions have raised additional questions. Beijing is counting on getting Taiwan back and is developing a military and naval force that will make it difficult for the United States to help Taiwan in a crisis. Land-based missiles like the DF-21 can attack U.S. carrier forces. Chinese submarines will seek to penetrate U.S. Navy battle groups. China is also building its own aircraft carriers. More recently, it has revived its territorial claims in the Pacific to the offshore Spratlys and Paracels and Sengaku (Diaoyu) islands. These historic claims were opposed by Japan, Vietnam, the Philippines, Brunei, and Korea, but China simply repeats its claims and will not negotiate with other parties. As a result, Japan, Korea, and Vietnam have moved closer to the United States economically and politically. Japan is no longer seeking to get the United States to evacuate its military presence on Okinawa. South Korea does not want its American troops to leave. Taiwan is concerned about its future. Hanoi is worried by the new militancy in Beijing. If Beijing further presses its territorial demands, it may create an anti-China phalanx in the Pacific region.

## Warring Camps

Asia today is like nineteenth-century Europe. European countries, competing with one another, became industrialized and formed even closer economic relations than exist in East Asia today. But they lacked close political ties. By 1907, Europe was split into two camps: the Triple Alliance against the Triple Entente. The economic interdependence between them was not sufficient to prevent war. In East Asia today, there is a great deal of trade in intermediate components and a number of locations for final assembly of products that will ultimately be exported to Western markets. Growth rates have risen and even countries like Cambodia, Bangladesh, and Laos are participating in the collective rise. But political relations are at a nadir, and the more aggressive China becomes in the South China Sea, the more it is leading many East Asian nations to renew their ties to the United States. In this important sense there is no united East to contrast or contend with the augmenting West. East Asia does not constitute an integrated entity. Divisions within the region are growing, not shrinking, and its economic growth is still tied to markets elsewhere in the world.

# THREE

# The Decline and Resurgence of the West

The financial crisis that gripped Europe in 2008–10 was caused by decades of overexpenditure on social services (extra-long vacations, short working weeks, overemployment in the governmental sector, early retirements) and undercollection of taxes. Greece, Italy, Spain, and Portugal were guilty on all counts, but the question was what to do about the problems they raised and represented. Should the European Central Bank, the International Monetary Fund, or strong E.U. countries like Germany and France simply bail them out? Would their own electorates accept retrenchment and cuts in social services along with tax increases? Would creditor nations give the needed money? The answer turned out to be "all of the above." Given its own indebtedness, the United States was hardly in a position to question European responses or to help solve the problem. America already had a deficit of $16 trillion that had not been remedied by tax hikes or cuts in expenditure (including needed defense cuts). While Europe was gradually coming to grips with its problems, the United States, paralyzed by impasse between Congress and the presidency, merely punted the ball. Debt limits forced temporary solutions but they did not last. On both sides of the Atlantic, the West was in deep crisis. Fortunately, however, economic growth stirred by government stimulus expenditure, borrowing, and lending opened a new vista of progress.

Historically, Europe and what became the United States were umbilically linked. The Americas, both North and South, were the progeny of Europe. The conquistadors changed the direction of Latin development, and the Pilgrims and their Virginia colleagues fashioned the religious and economic contours of North America. The native peoples who inhabited both realms were brushed aside as ships from Holland, England, and Spain beached on rocky and unpromising shores. In neither case did the European immigrants fully control events; they did, however, create a new political system that accepted close and initially subordinate relations with the mother country in Europe. Latin America, in thrall to Portugal and Spain, imbibed a form of European feudalism with prescribed social and ethnic ranks.[1] The later English settlers wished to get away from religious and economic controls in Europe and inaugurated a new system in North America. Reacting against royal excesses, the American colonists devised a system in which "checks and balances" cancelled concentrated authority. They believed the colonists could agree on most measures without the impetus of kingly or presidential fiat.

Though perhaps they would not put it in these terms, the uniqueness of their social situation made compromise both possible and likely. Different from European political systems,

North America had no caste or class distinctions between aristocracy, bourgeoisie, and worker-peasants. This followed from the migration that settled North America. Aristocracies rarely migrate, though the French *habitants* in Canada partook of the social system of Louis XIV. Farther south, those who escaped Europe were of middle-class stock: yeomanry, tradesmen, and shopkeepers who did not aim at social elevation. They wanted merely to excel in living standards and to exercise their religious preferences without hindrance. There was no aristocracy in middle-class America.[2] Conscious of their uniqueness (or what today would be called "exceptionalism"), Americans developed a contempt for or at least reserve toward still-feudal Europe. George Washington expressed it in his "fear of entangling alliances." And although he supported the French Revolution, Thomas Jefferson was equally concerned about contamination by European influences. This applied not only to the constant social conflict that characterized European social orders, but also to Europe's penchant for seemingly endless balance-of-power wars. In these international conflicts, Jefferson sympathized with the French, Hamilton with the English, but both feared too much American involvement with Europe. Weaker in power, the American nation could only preserve its uniqueness and social freedom by non-involvement, staying above the European fray.

Non-alignment and non-intervention reflected the most pessimistic American estimate of the European social order. Europeans, so Jefferson and Adams believed, could not create an American Constitution because they did not have socially equal Americans to create it.[3] European societies would never emerge in truly liberal form, or so Americans thought. Even wars would not transform Europe, at least not the War of 1812, in which British soldiers captured and burned Washington. Here the forefathers were probably wrong. After 1815, Europe's temporary return to the old ways belied the social and political progress that the Napoleonic Wars in fact represented. Liberalism was afoot, not only in France but in England, as both the Revolutions of 1830 and the great English Reform Act of 1832 demonstrated. The change also affected international relations, with Europe now poised between the Liberal Two (France and England) and the Conservative Three (Prussia, Russia, and Austria) under the ministrations of the Concert of Europe and Austria's Count Metternich. The liberalization of Europe proceeded through the Revolutions of 1848, but it was stopped by the conservative reaction in 1849 and afterward. Conservative, even aristocratic regimes used military force to keep their hold on power in Prussia, Austria and Russia; France installed a conservative form of Bonapartism under Napoleon III.

This reaction estranged the young American nation, which continued to assert its liberal credentials as territories became new states and the borders of the Union marched to the Pacific. The Civil War damaged American economic ties with Europe because it substituted Northern tariffs for the South's proclivity for low duties on trade. It reaffirmed U.S. influence morally, however, because the war made clear that America would now stand for equal rights for all its citizens, including the newly freed slaves. Britain had briefly considered intervening on the Southern side, but after the publication of *Uncle Tom's Cabin* and the outcry it gave rise to, London came down on the side of liberty and the American Union.

Full manhood suffrage was not attained until after 1890 in most European countries, and the lack of responsibility to parliament allowed ministers in Germany and other eastern states to neglect adverse minorities in the chamber.[4] The influence of the aristocracy remained paramount.[5]

In Western Europe the rise of socialists in France and Britain challenged liberal and middle-class parties, though the latter remained in power. This increased the differences with the United States, which continued to abhor socialism in all its forms. Labor and socialist parties in Europe, however, were not Marxist bomb-throwing conspirators, but rather ultimate bulwarks against the traditionalist and conservative parties. Louis Hartz contends that the United States never had a strong socialist movement because it did not have an aristocracy whose influence leftist parties had to overcome. American experience contradicted the common assumption that the regular procession of industrialism and technical development—with all of its urban degradation—would ultimately produce socialism.[6] In Europe it did do so, but perhaps because the nobility remained a continuing factor in politics. Aside from the brief popularity of Eugene Debs, who led a third-party alternative to Woodrow Wilson, socialism was anathema in the United States. Given Europe's aristocracy, socialism would occur on the Continent and would only begin to emulate middle-class parties when the nobility left the scene. This did not happen before 1914, but was a fact of life in Europe after 1945. Thus the full American rapprochement with Europe awaited the effects of the Second World War.

In the nineteenth and early twentieth centuries Europe and America also followed different economic paths. An agrarian nation, the United States sold its agriculture abroad with some success. But after the Civil War, America's high tariffs made it difficult for European industry to export to the United States in return. Rising American tariffs brought an industrial and financial elite to power, even though the United States was moving in a more progressive and populist direction. Nonetheless, American trade surpluses after 1874 created a mound of cash that could be loaned abroad. When the First World War occurred, Wall Street helped to bail out England and France. For the first time, under Woodrow Wilson, the United States forged closer links with Europe in political as well as economic realms. These ties were broken in 1919 with the Senate's rejection of the Versailles Treaty—including the League of Nations Covenant and the Treaty of Guarantee with France and England. This meant American interests in Europe had to be pursued through economic means. By buying German bonds after 1924, the United States helped float the liberal German republic, facilitating both payment of German reparations and also European repayment of debts to America. This triangle of payments continued until 1928, when the huge rise in the U.S. stock market rendered German bonds unattractive; without American loans, Germany began to founder. When the Great Depression hit in 1929, the United States did nothing to mitigate its impact in Europe; in fact, by raising tariffs and then devaluing the dollar, America made European recovery more difficult. The traditional exchange of U.S. farming exports for European industrial products was cancelled. Europe did not want the first and the United States did not want the second. Each side was using "beggar thy neighbor" policies against the other. While Nazi Germany and Imperial Japan rearmed to change the world balance, the United States and Western Europe maneuvered for partisan advantage, thereby splintering the West.

This changed after World War II. By then the United States

had become the capital abundant zone, and Europe was temporarily relegated to "labor abundance," because of its unemployment. But after 1958 and the establishment of convertible currencies, each lowered tariffs on the goods of the other—the United States because it helped to design the products that Europe produced, Europe because it needed American technology and markets. Instead of exchanges of agriculture for industry, both sides protected agriculture and engaged in intra-industry specialization and trade. Different types of automobiles, chemicals, pharmaceuticals, and luxury goods were sold by each side. Both benefited from the outcome, but the developing world could not sell primary produce in either Western market. Harnessing their labor abundance, however, rising states could manufacture goods designed in the West. In addition, foreign direct investment between America and Europe allowed each to make sophisticated goods in the other's backyard.

Thus it took a century and a half for the new American nation to fashion close relations with European colleagues. The Cold War with the Soviet Union also brought the two halves of the West together. Foreign direct investment solidified the political connection, as the European Union placed $1.3 trillion in the United States, and America $1.4 trillion in Europe.

## The Resurgence of Europe
The European Union represents a new experiment in political life. By combining twenty-seven states (twenty-eight, when Iceland joins), the European Union has improved both its security and its economic potential. When one remembers the nineteenth- and twentieth-century clashes between Britain and Germany, Germany and France, and between all of them and Russia, a pessimist might expect the violence between

European countries to rise once again. Actually, however, the European Union has put traditional balance-of-power wars behind it. Having become a peaceful power, Europe has found a way of growing in place without attacking anybody else. Unlike past political empires, Europe has made itself so attractive that more states want to join it. Robert Mundell, the father of the euro (and the author of a key work on optimum currency areas), predicted several years ago that the European Union and the euro currency zone would ultimately grow to embrace fifty countries.[7] The basis for such a breathtaking forecast was that other nations would find growth within the common currency area greater than they would gain outside it.

Crisis was the mother of invention in this respect. In 1945, European leaders began to recognize that, as disunited independent states, they could not compete on an equal basis with the United States or the Soviet Union—two continental-sized powers with hundreds of millions of citizens. Jean Monnet, a hitherto obscure broker from Cognac, convinced his French and later German colleagues that European states could redress their relationship with the two superpowers only if they came together. This inaugurated the historic compromise between Germany and France to construct Europe. Along with Robert Schuman, Monnet started the process of integration leading to unity. It's likely that neither foresaw that the idea would be as successful as it's been: the present twenty-seven states will shortly be joined by up to ten others, with the European Union reaching nearly to the Caucasus.

Despite historic precedents, Europe's integration has not been designed to create another imperial state with the trappings of traditional grandeur. Instead of pounding on the table, Europe glides into the room. The Single European Act (which defined a large open market) passed nearly unnoticed in 1986. The Maastricht Treaty of 1992 was more controversial. It rendered the European Community into a Union, provided for common judicial standards and an agreement on immigration, and adumbrated the first steps toward a common foreign policy. In 1998 these were codified in setting up a representative to help formulate the European Union's common security and foreign policy. Also in 1998 the union introduced a new currency—the euro, adopted by sixteen states—and created a European Central Bank to set monetary policy for those joining the eurozone. The 2003 Nice Treaty (formulated to adjust to the twenty-five members then in the union or in the process of joining) introduced qualified majority decision making. Member states accounting for at least 62 percent of the union's population have to favor all qualified majority decisions, and such decisions will inevitably play a larger role over time. The Lisbon Treaty broadened qualified majority voting, set up a permanent president of the council, and appointed a high representative for foreign affairs and security policy, amending the Nice Treaty.

The European Union is a supranational unit in the sense that it has acquired large powers from its constituent member states but has not become a federal union in constitutional terms. Neither the European Commission nor the Council of Ministers enjoys the powers of a federal executive body. The European Union is a partial merger in which members still retain influence and must be consulted for further integration to occur. In corporate terms it is more like Renault's equal merger with Nissan than Walmart's swallowing up of one key supplier. Britain and France cannot dictate to Germany. European integration, furthermore, is as much legal as it is political, and the

European Court can invalidate legislation or decisions in areas of its jurisdiction.[8] While national legislatures retain authority on taxes, defense, and welfare, European institutions govern individual rights, trade, monetary policy, the environment, and ultimately foreign policy. European institutions make sure that governments are following the *acquis communautaire*, or cumulative body of E.U. law, by carefully monitoring developments within each state. Surveillance ultimately leads to compliance, and openness provides the basis for supervision. The role of the European Commission is unique. Whereas normal states make policy with a day-to-day perspective, the European Commission in Brussels adopts a long-term view. It asks what the ultimate shape of Europe should be. It questions the future of competition, finance, and trade. European commissioners have an ability to plan ahead that few of their national counterparts enjoy.

In practical terms the European Union has proceeded from a common market area (established in 1957) to a common currency and monetary policy colossus in 1999–2000. And the currency it created—the euro—has risen quickly in relation to the American dollar. At each stage of greater market integration, critics proclaimed that the new level could not be sustained or would lead to the defection of members.[9] Yet enlargement and integration have proceeded simultaneously. A "multi-speed Europe," in which some members could proceed faster or more slowly than others on specific issues, made this possible. In finance, seventeen countries are members of the euro; in immigration, fifteen have agreed to labor mobility without passport controls; ten have forged a common defense effort.

The prospective and actual admission of Eastern European

and former Soviet republics like Ukraine, Moldova, Belarus, and the already admitted Baltic states will create a market and source of low-cost production that did not exist previously, as Europe begins, however glacially, to move into Asia. In 1905 the famous British geographer Halford Mackinder denominated western Russia as the European heartland.[10] He claimed: "Who rules East Europe commands the Heartland. Who rules the Heartland commands the World-Island [of Eurasia], and who rules the World-Island commands the World." This formula was modified in 1944 by an American geopolitician, Nicholas Spykman. Spykman focused on the Rimland—the western and island glacis surrounding the Heartland. He believed control of the Rimland was more important than the Heartland, which was no more than an arid and vacant steppe. The Rimlands include Western Europe, the British Isles, India, coastal China, Japan, and by extension the United States. Today, the (European) Rimland is enlisting and converting the (Russian and Central Asian) Heartland to its mode of political and economic existence (figure 1).[11]

This is a geopolitical feat of first importance. It could occur in Europe because France and Germany, abetted by Britain, have made a historic compromise. The founding of a cooperative core of key powers attracted others to join. Clyde Prestowitz, by no means a traditional Europhile, writes: "The European Union is a single, increasingly powerful entity. It comprises [27] countries with a combined population of [499] million and a GDP of [$16.3] trillion—compared with the U.S. population of [307] million and a GDP of [$14.1] trillion. In addition to being the world's largest economy, the EU is also the largest trader of goods and services. It has a president, a parliament, a [draft] constitution, a cabinet, a central bank,

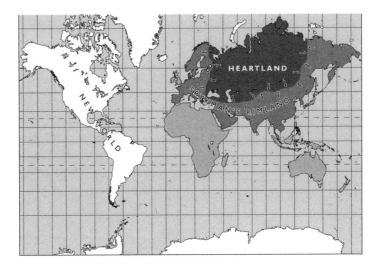

Figure 1. Heartland and Rimland
(Adapted by Bill Nelson from Mark Polelle, *Raising Cartographic Conscious-
ness: The Social and Foreign Policy Vision of Geopolitics in the Twentieth Century,*
Lanham, Md.: Lexington Books, 1999)

a currency, a bill of rights, a unified patent office, a court system with power to override any national court, embassies and
ambassadors around the globe, a 60,000-member army independent of NATO or any outside authority, a space agency
with 200 satellites in orbit including its own spy satellites, a
flag, an anthem, and a national day. Citizens of Europe use a
standard license plate and carry standard birth certificates and
passports."[12]

Europe did not achieve this position smoothly. There were
fits and starts, failures and successes. Six powers joined the European Common Market in 1957, but after Charles de Gaulle
became president of France in 1958, progress was intermit-
tent. In 1962 he imposed a veto on British membership that

endured until 1973. In 1965, European integration ground to a halt after France refused to meet with the Council of Ministers. When Georges Pompidou succeeded De Gaulle in 1969, however, he relented, and the United Kingdom was admitted to the European Community in 1973 along with Ireland and Denmark. At the same time, the group agreed to a common external tariff, not just internal free trade.

In 1979 the European monetary system was set up, which restricted fluctuation of national currencies to 2.5 percent in regard to a standard currency, in this case the Deutsche mark. England and Italy were members. In 1992 neither Italy nor Britain could keep its currency aligned with the Deutsche mark (which was overvalued), and they both withdrew. Later Italy rejoined a modified EMS that allowed fluctuations up to 15 percent. After the euro was created in 1999, seventeen countries eventually renounced their own issue and joined the common currency. At each step, the European Union reached a higher level of integration.

After its creation in 1957, the European Community expanded in two phases. In the 1970s, Portugal, Spain, and Greece ended their autocratic regimes and successfully applied for membership, which was granted in 1981. Then, starting in 1989, former members of the Soviet bloc were admitted, along with nations that had been neutral in the Cold War: Austria, the Czech Republic, Finland, and Sweden, and later Cyprus, Hungary, Poland, Slovakia, Latvia, Lithuania, Estonia, and Malta. In 2005 Romania, Bulgaria, and Slovenia also joined, bringing the total to twenty-seven.[13] The growth in membership was accompanied by increased integration, with free movement of persons, full free trade, and a common currency. In the second decade of the twenty-first century, the waiting list included Turkey, Croatia, Serbia, Montenegro, Macedonia, and Iceland, with the Caucasus states looming in the background.

Europe cannot expand forever. Still, the euro as a single currency becomes more influential as the base of countries using it expands. Outsiders want to diminish transaction costs and increase inward investment. Insiders want their currency used more generally, increasing its acceptability and reducing the need for higher interest rates to make it attractive. The nature of the good in question—particularly if it is a club good and reserved to members[14]—can assist the continuing expansion of the club.[15]

There is another important reason for the European Union's continuing expansion. Under Vladimir Putin, Russia has tried to reenlist the former Soviet republics in its orbit. Ukraine, Kazakhstan, Belarus, Armenia, and Azerbaijan will be lured back into Greater Russia if the European Union continues to rebuff eastern applicants. They all know they must make greater progress in democratic politics to join, but democracy is not attractive to all leaders. Alliance with Russia offers these leaders an alternative, which means that E.U. membership—or the realistic prospect of it—is necessary for the further expansion of democratic governance into Central Asia. These applicants know that Russia cannot offer the economic benefits that Europe does, and also that Moscow may seek to undermine their security.

## Reversing the Balance of Power

Europe can succeed in part because it needs less defense protection. Why is that? It is because an unparalleled transformation has allowed Europe to reverse the impact of the balance of power on its frontiers. Historically, enlarging and economically centralizing units generally attracted opposition, not support. As Germany united and centralized in the second half of the nineteenth century, for instance, it raised not blessings but fears. French power and Napoleonic ambitions were not welcome. Later, Hitler's ruthless machinations to expand German territory ultimately led to strong opposition. But today Europe's peaceful growth and centralization have created only converts, not opponents; outsiders are standing in line not to oppose but to join. The accumulation of power no longer repels; it is beginning to attract. The agglomerating power of Brussels (even though this seems an oxymoron) has occasioned no opposition whatever. The United States, which some view as a potential rival to an integrated Europe, has encouraged European enlargement and sought to speed it up.

Many Americans explain that because Europe is a peaceful power with no geopolitical ambitions, nearby political units can trust it. Europe has yet no foreign policy decision-making center. If the president of the United States telephoned the president of the council, the high representative for foreign policy, or the head of the European Commission, he would not find out precisely what European policy was. The president would also have to ask the European Council and key national leaders, and there might not be a single agreed policy. With such possible discord, it is said, Europe cannot throw its weight around in the councils of the world. That is why no one worries when Europe unites: only economic unity is involved, and sometimes not even that.

This is of course true, but it is oversimple. As critics of neo-realism have argued, power does not determine intentions.[16] Europe could have great power—and even a united decision-making apparatus—and still not present a threat, because its intentions are peaceful to nearby states and the outside world. The peace expressed inside the union (bringing power together) would also be expressed outside the union (bringing others in).

There is another and more important reason why Europe's unification does not raise hackles. There is an intrinsic difference between economic power and political power. Economically, the rise of one center of strength tends to benefit those close to it. Assuming a degree of openness, capital, demand, and incomes rise in consequence of the growth of a nearby economy. Thus while political power brings fragmentation, economic strength has a centralizing effect. The natural tendency of thriving markets is to get larger, capital to augment, and consumption to increase. Migration moves toward the stronger economic pulse. Only if there are artificial political barriers does this not occur. A strong economic drive to unity can weaken the barriers to political association, as we are seeing between Taiwan and mainland China today.

European modernity has moved to a new stage in which power and force have run up against their limits. In this stage, in Stephen Toulmin's words, "the name of the game will be influence, not force."[17] Europe is no longer a military Leviathan, but its soft power is the marvel of the world. No national or rising superstate can compare with it.

Despite the ups and downs of individual countries, European success has moved steadily forward. But Europe did not recover quickly from the great recession of 2008–10. Growth rates fell and unemployment rose to 9 percent. Countries could not agree to accept further immigration; some wanted controls on the mobility of labor within the union. They disagreed on monetary and fiscal policy, with Germany pressing for higher interest rates and cuts in government spending while weaker nations like Greece and Spain were still disbursing unsustainable amounts of cash. This raised the question: should Europe become a "fiscal union" in which monetary transfers from one rich country compensate for a weaker nation's overexpenditure? Or should each European ship keep itself afloat? Surplus earners are as much at fault as debtors, but the European Union had not yet decided to give the council or the European Central Bank authority over individual nations' budgets. In December 2011, however, the union agreed to hold national deficits to 0.5 percent of GDP. Therefore, in practical terms, the ECB and strong members like Germany and France have met to resolve each crisis, even though they have no formal obligation or authority to do so.[18] The December 2011 agreement also lays the foundation for ECB action to buy bonds of member nations, lowering their interest rates and keeping them within the eurozone. While the ECB's role has been largely limited to de facto management of each new crisis, each setback ends up giving new powers to the European Union.

## Japan—Can It Be Part of the West?

The integration of Europe and its increasing ties to the United States raise another question: can the West be extended further? The political and economic linkage between Europe and America suggests that other major industrial nations with a similar political relationship to the United States could also join the West. Can Japan do so?

Japan is located nearly 135 degrees east of the prime meridian, situating it directly in Asia. Yet in the past fifty years it has modified and partly transcended its Asian heritage, linking it now more closely to the West in both democratic and industrial terms. This does not mean that Japan is socially Western; it retains its Buddhist and Shinto orientations, and it is still a "vertical society" in the words of Chie Nakane, Japan's most profound anthropologist. The top dictates to the bottom in social terms. Japanese also learn to speak three languages: one to equals, one to inferiors, and another to high-ranking individuals. Social relations do not work unless and until reciprocal status can be sorted out. When it is, however, Japan forms a more united nation than is typically found in most of the Western world.

Of course, Japan has always been ethnically united; it consisted of a relatively uniform blending of Asian peoples with an admixture of Caucasian traits and lighter skins found in the northerly islands of Hokkaido, not far from Russia. Before it opened to the West in the 1850s Japan had an already effective if traditional economy. Because feudal lords (samurai) had to travel to Edo (Tokyo) to meet their obligations to the shogun every other year, roads were improved, post houses set up, and food provided for the travelers. Administrative skills developed to ensure their safe arrival. This arrangement meant (as in Louis XIV's France) that feudal lords could not consolidate powerful positions in the countryside from which to challenge the political center.[19] Iron mines, financial capital (in Osaka), and craft industries sprang up long before the West's military intrusion in 1853. As an island people, the Japanese had worried about foreign invasion and had concentrated together to prevent it. They were preternaturally ready to react when Admiral Matthew Perry's black ships steamed into Tokyo Bay and demanded that Japan open to the outside world.

After Perry left, the Japanese reinstituted the emperor's sway, and the Meiji restoration of his powers took place in 1868. Thereafter economic growth went even faster, rivaling Germany and England. Japan knew it needed a high-performance industrial economy if it was to ward off attack from Russia and the West.

In many ways the policy of Japan is the weathervane of international politics. After the Industrial Revolution had worked itself out in the body of European nineteenth-century politics, Arnold Toynbee thought that industrialism would triumph over nationalism. It did not: instead, territorial aggression came to the fore. Japan led the pack with its attack on China in 1894 and Russia a decade later. Even its military tactics foreshadowed those used in the First World War. In the 1930s, before Italy and Germany invaded others, Japan had already occupied Manchuria and begun a war with China. In both cases other powers followed in its wake. After its defeat in the Pacific war, Japan reversed course and led a world trend in the opposite direction. Long before the Johnny-come-lately Great Powers (the United States and the Soviet Union) understood what was going on, Japan had already put into practice the strategy of the trading state. Eschewing militarism, it forged a new path of economic development, stimulated by foreign commerce. Then in the 1990s Japan's industrial stagnation neatly prefigured the later American and European recessions. Japan's near collapse after 1987 should have warned the world of the dangers ahead.

Today Japan has reached a similar choice point in which it may well chart another new course for the world. It has enhanced its democracy with a new two-party structure; it has moved some of its productive apparatus to the United States and China and specialized in high-tech innovations in cars, biotechnology, and robotics. But while trading with all countries, Japan has seen to it that its political relationships with the West are on firm ground.[20] Japan cannot prosper in a divided world that oscillates between Islamic religiosity on one hand and rational administration on the other—trade, investment, and commerce of all kinds require trust and predictability. Provided by the West, these cannot be found in an international system beset by global uncertainty. Even during the Cold War, the stability of bipolarity at least provided an open half of the world with which to trade. If Japan is to succeed today, it needs a "new" West to provide leadership and order in markets and political relationships.

Japan, however, learned a lapidary lesson from America's victory in the Second World War: Tokyo would not be able to prevail militarily against the West but had in a sense to join the Western group economically to succeed. I can remember asking an official of the Foreign Ministry who was conducting me to Kyoto whether Japan had any postwar problems. He said they did until 1952, when the Japanese people "got their national goal," which was to emulate and then equal the performance of Western industrial economies.

The rise of China and the resurgence of Islam have contributed to Japan's new sense that it belongs in the Western camp where economic intercourse offsets the travails of Middle Eastern chaos and Chinese territorial claims. In recent years and in social terms, Japan has also moved to the two-parent nuclear family as opposed to China's extended family system. Parents cling to their children and obligations are mutual, but they do not necessarily involve more distant relationships. Japanese have also learned the benefits from recruiting meritocratic "outsiders" in industry and commerce and become a country with a high degree of social trust. Unlike Italy and even China, Japanese enterprises are not family businesses; nor are they run by the government. Highly trained experts manage most of them. Japanese business is also concentrated, with the top twenty firms representing 10 percent of all employment, with keiretsu relationships among them.[21] All major Japanese firms are in such relationships, and they buy from each other, rather than from foreign companies, even where price or quality might dictate otherwise.[22] The Japanese computer industry was in its infancy in the 1980s; it still bought little from IBM, the world's leading producer, because Japan preferred less efficient (but closely connected) domestic producers.

After its defeat in World War II, Japan resolved to rise from its diminished position and to master the most complicated civilian industries and export sophisticated products to developed citadels of the United States and Europe. Stimulated by U.S. procurement orders during the Korean War, Japanese firms set up electronics and enhanced automotive production and moved into machine tools. Initially these firms focused on manufacturing of Western-invented devices, like the tape recorder. But later Japan's corporations devised their own products and created just-in-time production systems, robotics, quality circles (instead of production lines), highly refined cars and trucks, and consumer electronics. For the decade of the 1960s, Japan grew at 10 percent per year. Later—until 1987—it settled for 4 percent. But it progressively began to dominate the world trade in industrial goods.

## The Crisis of 1989

Japan's success was at least partly based on the connection between its domestic industrial and property markets: the two rose in tandem. Land values escalated continually, to the point where in 1987, all the land in the state of California was valued at less than the grounds of the Imperial Palace in Tokyo. Everyone assumed that land and housing prices would continue to increase because Japanese labor and capital were coming into the Tokyo metropolitan area. Corporations held land; stocks were combinations of industrial and property assets. But on December 25, 1989, the head of the central bank, Yasushi Mieno, decided that the rise of the Nikkei index from 10,000 to nearly 40,000 yen was a bubble that had to be lanced. By raising interest rates by 1.75 percent on that Christmas Day, Mieno caused a free fall in the stock market, which also entailed a later collapse of the Japanese housing market. Investors who had believed that property values could not go down were totally unprepared for the crash. In the 1990s, many Japanese home and apartment owners discovered that their property was now worth less than their mortgages.

Japan had always maintained a high savings rate—which Japanese savers attributed to the lack of a full social security and pension system. This also reduced consumption. Domestic demand was low. When interest rates went up and housing values down, consumption fell still more, taking with it the typical 4 percent Japanese rate of growth. Through the 1990s Japan averaged only about 1 percent growth per year. In response, a succession of Japanese governments offered stimulus packages, sometimes building "bridges to nowhere," but these did not fully right the economic ship. They did, however, put the government so deeply in debt that interest rates could not fall further. The government even increased consumption taxes to remedy the situation, but this only further depressed growth. Not until the turn of the century did Japan begin to emerge from its fiscal morass of non-performing mortgage loans. Domestic consumption finally rose, but it was cut by the huge recession after 2008. Another bout of belt tightening followed.

Nonetheless, Japanese politics opened up, and the LDP (Liberal-Democratic Party), which had been in office for a half century, gave way to the Democratic Party of Japan (DPJ) and to a series of prime ministers seeking to reshape Japan's external policy. Because of its rivalry with China, which has now passed Japan to become the second largest economy after the United States, Tokyo has solidified its relationships with America and India and invested in a satellite and space program. Japan has also sought to improve its economic relationship with China, which now receives more Japanese exports than does the United States. These are not primarily finished goods but components to be assembled in China and sent back to Japan or to markets in the United States and Europe. China's finished-goods exports are primarily directed not to Asia but rather to the West.

Japan has tried to strengthen its relationship with America in a variety of ways. It continues to fabricate the last stage of many of its finished goods in southern and midwestern American states, providing employment for U.S. workers. Internationally, Tokyo has improved its relations with Washington and moved to greater defense cooperation, implicitly directed against China. It has denied Beijing's territorial claims in the South China Sea while accepting U.S. proposals for an antimissile system that might protect Japan as well as Taiwan. Closer Japanese links with NATO are on the horizon.

In the longer term, Japan's aging and declining population will pose great difficulties for the world's third industrial nation. It can compensate only by joining forces with the West in both political and economic terms to offset China's rise and its own decline.

## The United States

The strengths and weaknesses of the United States of America are different. Unlike Europe, the United States is formally united and does constitute a fiscal union, with the federal government able and sometimes ready to help the states. It has power to act on all the contentious issues: social security, health care, immigration, defense spending, and taxes—but it does not always do so. These failures represent gaps in the American constitutional system that still need to be filled.

In the 1950s, the political theorist and historian Louis Hartz argued that America's difficulties in part stemmed from its founding. In the seventeenth and eighteenth centuries, migrants to America came from middle-class stock in their countries of origin, leaving the aristocracy and the proletariat at home.[23] Social divisions in the United States were therefore less than they had been in England, France, or Germany. Americans had income differences, but they were not divided socially into working class, middle class, and nobility. Given this greater social unity, the founding fathers believed that they did not need a rigorously centralized or hierarchic political system that might repeat the errors of the British monarchy. They also believed that decentralizing and separating power would prevent any particular faction from asserting control. They thus wrote a constitution that created no final source of authority—certainly no king. Instead they separated power among executive, legislative, and judicial branches, and divided it as well between the federal government and the states. The framers could accept a Constitution that depended upon social agreement on the basic political objectives and means to achieve them because they thought cooperation would always be forthcoming.

This cooperation worked relatively well in the early years of the republic, though margins of decision were often close. Jefferson was elected president in 1800 by only one vote in the electoral college; Andrew Jackson was deprived of the presidency in 1824 even though he had the popular vote on his side, as did Samuel Tilden in 1876;[24] the declaration of war against Mexico in 1846 was passed by only one vote. In more recent years Bill Clinton's tax increase in 1993 was passed by the House of Representatives by just one vote. In the Senate, Bob Kerrey's vote in favor effectively ended his political career.

In recent years the drumbeat of opposition has become more insistent. Senators and representatives fly home on weekends; they socialize together much less, and informal compromise has suffered. Many Republicans have signed the Grover Norquist pledge against new taxes, even those involved in closing blatant loopholes. The old analysis of Anthony Downs that suggested that candidates would moderate their positions and move toward the center to get the largest number of votes has turned out not to be true.[25] Instead, candidates take extreme positions, but still can rely on political action committee support from wealthy partisans whose money gives them television time and funds for political attack ads against opponents. The Supreme Court's decision in the *Citizens United* case means that few if any limits can be placed on campaign contributions. Even candidates far to the right can present themselves effectively to voters if they have enough money and television time.

As a result, major divisions have grown up within and between legislative bodies, between Congress and the presidency, and between the federal government and the states. In the Senate, the vastly increased use of the filibuster seems to demand supermajority agreement on issues that should be routine. A Congress held by one party can impose its veto on a presidency held by another. An American government increasingly riven by conflict finds it harder and harder to act, even in situations (such as raising the government's debt limit) where action was once routine.

The increasing inequality of the American electorate has made institutional compromise more difficult. As Robert Reich shows, there have been three recent periods in which wealth either accumulated in fewer hands or was distributed more evenly to the American population. From 1913 to 1929 the top 1 percent of American earners took an increasing proportion of the national income, rising to 24 percent in 1929. Beginning with the Great Depression and the New Deal, that proportion declined until it reached a low of 9 percent in 1978. With Reagan and his successors, however, the wealthy took more and more of the social product, rising to 23 percent in 2007. That rise, however, was unsustainable. By their purchases, the richest 1 percent cannot stimulate the economy and produce enough growth for the remaining 99 percent, even though their average income in 2007 was \$713,000.[26] The rich do not spend all their money, while the poor borrow in order to spend more than they have. For the United States to progress, money must be given back to those who will disburse it and consume in large amounts.[27] It is not surprising that important wealthy Americans like Warren Buffett have called for higher taxes on themselves. In time, tax reform will begin to bring this about.

This would not mean, however, that America has transcended the historical problem of rise and decline of major nations. Historically, there is an escalator up and an elevator down. All Great Powers have eventually been forced to yield the baton to rising nations, through war or deficient economic growth. In the past, Portugal gave way to Holland; Holland to England; England to Germany; Germany to Russia; and Russia to the United States. Thomas Friedman and Michael Mandelbaum claim that America can forever remain the single exceptional nation.[28] This is not possible, however; in time it will proffer the scepter of primacy to China. According to *The Hill*, in October 2011, 69 percent of Americans thought the United States was in decline.[29] Meanwhile, 46 percent think China either will replace or has already replaced the United States as the world's leading superpower.[30]

Could America come back? Since the days of the founding fathers, American politics has become more divided; whatever social similarity existed at the republic's founding has been eroded away by economic and political splits between higher and lower income strata. Inequality now divides the United States politically as well as economically. In Congress, the filibuster—merely a Senate-adopted voting rule, not required by the Constitution—ensures that well-financed special interests can prevent change. A Great Depression like that of 1929–39 can bring politics back together. So can a major war. But such situations neither are desirable nor seem likely. The American recovery from the recent recession has been just sufficient to prevent wholesale reform of both the tax and expenditure systems. The wars in Afghanistan and Iraq, together with the threat from Iran, have slid by a partly unnoticing American public. None of these occasioned a coming together of Americans to undertake new and difficult tasks. The United States has not yet experienced large, decisive, and continuing failure. Like President Calvin Coolidge, President Barack Obama has been able to skate over the cracks in the pavement, bringing most of the U.S. public with him. The short-term budget deficit and absolutely necessary expenditure cuts have preoccupied the public, while longer-term issues like the rise of China, the pervasive incapacity of the U.S. economy to be resurrected, and the ultimate challenge of the energy crisis have been shunted aside. With all the problems accumulating, the United States was temporarily paralyzed. Each problem's solution would make others worse. Large cuts in defense would rip a hole in America's long-term deterrence. Large cuts in entitlements, meaning Medicare and Social Security, would devastate incomes and reduce demand. Cuts in pensions would make it much harder for parents to send their children to college. Taking the energy crisis seriously would mean a carbon tax and a slowdown in growth previously supported by fossil fuels.

All of these things could actually be done, but not by a business-as-usual electorate. Americans' lives changed during World War II, and people willingly made the sacrifices necessary to save the nation. Few Americans want to make additional financial sacrifices today; they already need two parents working to pay for their children's needs. Single-parent families have no extra money.

Yet we know nations can come back. After Hiroshima and

Nagasaki, the Japanese people rebuilt their country and entered a new and more dynamic industrial age. After the Allied invasion and conquest of Germany, German citizens pressed on, creating a vibrant economy and a new European Union to bring Europe together and to assuage their deeply felt consciousness of guilt about the Second World War. Americans can still revive their nation, but they can't do it alone. Just as Europe's revival after 1945 depended on American help, so U.S. revival depends on European and Japanese help. While Japan is aging, both Europe and America are genteelly slipping into the cisterns of history. European growth rates are 1.5 percent, the U.S. perhaps 2 percent. With Chinese expansion of 5–7 percent or more, it will not be long before China seizes its rightful place in the pantheon of nations, at the top. Deng Xiaoping's injunction not to make waves may well be jettisoned by new leaders.[31]

A new Western union, however, casting an unbreakable cable across the Atlantic, and then linking with Japan, could change this negation. The cable should be connected to a powerful winch that could draw the continents closer still. In no three regions of the world is democracy and the rule of law so well established as in America, Europe, and now Japan. Nowhere else does educational preparation so well gird individuals for industrial, economic, and professional occupations and for the international competition that follows from excellence. Nowhere else does culture partner with technology to create innovations that are both attractive and precise, like the BMW automobile, the Telaferique cable car in Switzerland, the ravishing gown in Milan, the iPad in Silicon Valley, the Japanese creation of humanoid robots. It is no accident that the West has developed the marvelous new products of the past ten years, while countries in the East assemble them. Along the new frontiers of genetics, optics, and biotechnology, diseases can not only be controlled—in theory human DNA can be improved.[32] What is critical for the United States, Europe, and Japan, however, is the partnership in innovation, finance, and high-level manufacture that leads the world. American capitalism is already highly invested in Europe, as is Japanese technology in the United States. Europe has repaid the favor in spades, acquiring and building capacity in North America. The three capitalisms link together, hand into glove. The Atlantic combination is particularly strong. The companies of Europe and the United States have engaged in a giant merger. Is it not time for the countries also to do so? Even the land and seascape of the geographic borders meld into one another as they did geologically in past historic time. This was the intercontinental Jurassic Union of 150 million years ago (figure 2).

## West Reunited

Despite differences among its parts, the second decade of the twenty-first century is likely to witness a progressive reunification of the West. This will happen for economic, military, and cultural reasons. Economically, growth in both Europe and America is shallow. Europe's major economies have subsisted on export-led growth. France, Germany, Holland, Belgium, and Switzerland have prospered because of their intricate and high-tech exports. They have sold some of these products (about 65 percent) to one another, but an increasing proportion now goes overseas to the United States, Japan, and China. Europe used to do about 80 percent of its trade with itself; now it does 35 percent with the outside world, and that proportion is increasing. Of these exports, about 11 percent goes to the United

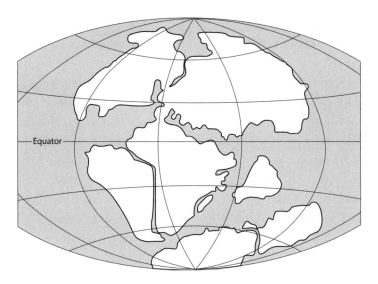

Figure 2. Jurassic linkage of Europe and North America
(150 million years ago)
(Adapted by Bill Nelson from the U.S. Geological Survey,
Department of the Interior/USGS)

States. The United States has been the European Union's most important trading partner, a relationship that is unlikely to change.

Both the United States and Europe are predisposed to extend their customs unions to each other in the next decade. America has concluded free-trade agreements with Canada, Mexico, South Korea, Colombia, and Panama. It will wish to increase its benefits further by selling in a larger free-trade zone. The European Union has negotiated trade preference arrangements with Mexico, and is seeking agreements with the Association of South East Asian Nations (ASEAN), several Central American countries, South Korea, and India. More than 50 percent of world trade now takes place within such trade preference zones. Such unions allow increasing returns to scale, help to equalize domestic prices, and move the globe toward worldwide free trade.[33]

A customs union between the United States and Europe would be a beacon for the world. The American tariff on imported manufactured goods is only about 2 percent, and the E.U. tariff about 3 percent. On the other hand, foodstuffs and many services are not included in this calculation. Non-tariff barriers are still so high that the European Commission estimates that a mutual removal of all non-tariff barriers would increase annual E.U. growth by 0.7 percent and increase U.S. growth by 0.3 percent, leading to increases in GDP respectively of $53 billion and $158 billion in one year. Just as it did in 1948, a closer military-political and economic relationship between the United States and Europe would stimulate greater investment on both sides. The two great economic units are already the world's largest trading partners by a very wide margin.[34]

But size is not the only reason for stronger U.S.-European economic ties. Customs unions, while they bring specified member countries together, also discriminate against those left outside. Increasingly there will be reason to gain leverage against countries in Asia that have not opened their markets or adjusted their currencies sufficiently to remedy huge trade imbalances. Nothing on the horizon suggests an agreement to let capital move freely in or out of China; there is also no consensus on raising the value of the renminbi. As the imbalances accumulate, both Europe and the United States would like to induce China to move to a policy of greater balance. They can do this more effectively if they pursue a coordinated strategy.

Thus a customs union between the United States and the European Union will become increasingly attractive as the Asian nations grow. In August 1971, Treasury Secretary John Connally, facing inaction from trading partners, placed a temporary 10 percent surcharge on trade with the rest of the world. Before that, neither Japan nor Germany had been willing to raise the value of their currencies to restore equilibrium with the United States. After he did so, their currencies rose automatically as the dollar depreciated by 10 percent in 1971 and a total of 30 percent in 1973. A larger common market including the United States and Europe within a single customs zone would exert similar pressure on Beijing, raising de facto tariffs in both the United States and Europe and lowering the value of both the dollar and the euro. Even if these tariffs are only temporary, they will have a galvanic effect leading toward economic balance between the two Western powers and China.

Politically, the United States and Europe have moved closer together. This is not only because their leaderships now see international and economic matters from a common point of view; it is also because the trend of events internationally suggests a shift of power to the East that needs to be equilibrated. Major issues with China have not been solved. There is no agreement on an economic balance; there is no military agreement that would stabilize and limit forces on both sides; there is no territorial agreement, with China now claiming sovereignty over the nearby islands in the South China Sea; there is no agreement to limit greenhouse gas emissions. Economic and strategic specialists troop between Beijing and Washington, but no cooperation is actually achieved. One remembers that it was the failure of negotiations to limit the German

High Seas Fleet in 1912 (the Haldane Mission) that played into the tension that led to World War I between Britain and Germany two years later.

Germany today plays a role in relations among Western nations not seen since the nineteenth century. Chancellor Angela Merkel has moved her country into a position within the West that is as central as Bismarck's was in years past. Politically, Germany is the linchpin that holds other Europeans together, bringing France and Italy toward a stronger focus on Eastern Europe, where Poland, once Germany's enemy, has now for the first time accepted greater German initiative. Merkel is a fiscal conservative who believes that growth depends on market approval of government policy and that reining in debts will spur private investment. Her economic policy resembles Bill Clinton's. In 1996 Clinton's treasury secretary, Robert Rubin, stressed a "bond market theory" of growth that would favor low interest rates and rapid payment of fiscal obligations (or even running surpluses) to increase stock and property values. Economic growth and greater productivity would follow, and they did in rapid succession. Merkel's experiment is being closely watched by Russia and China. Though it may be premature to say so, Merkel's influence in keeping Europe together also resembles Bismarck's. The Iron Chancellor made sure that Austria and Italy always sided with Germany. More important, he also guaranteed that the wider world of Eastern and Western Europe—Russia and Britain in particular—would support Germany's central role, thereby ensuring a broader peace. Colonial rivalries would not lead to war as long as Bismarck's central coalition held together. When that failed after 1890, imperial aggressiveness in North Africa and Eastern Europe were no longer balanced by Bismarck's central control. Left to fester, they brought Russia to fight with Austria in 1914, collapsing the continent in world war. Merkel, however, continues to "hold the ring." She will bring the United States in just as Bismarck brought England in.

After 2011, the balance of power began to come into existence to counterbalance Chinese gains. One side in this balance is the disunited East. The United States and Europe, sustained by common agreement on NATO, will be the balancers. Recently President Obama wrote: "The European Union is America's single largest economic partner and a critical anchor of the global economy. I am confident that Europe has the financial and economic capacity to meet this challenge, and the United States will continue to support our European partners as they work to resolve this crisis."[35]

The final factor joining Europe and the United States is cultural. America and Europe share the classical traditions that gave rise to Western values. The Greek worlds of Philip of Macedon and his son Alexander the Great, Athens and Sparta, the historic perspectives of Thucydides, the philosophic ones of Aristotle and Plato—all these undergird Western civilization. The American founding fathers, including George Washington, Thomas Jefferson, and Alexander Hamilton, were steeped in classical lore and influenced by the French Revolution. They cited William Wordsworth and Montesquieu in their construction of a new society. Appreciating democratic peoples, Dickens and Tocqueville also became ideological kinsmen of the New World. Today, despite occasional American lapses, the United States and Western Europe continue to share common values and interests.

With the onset of globalization, liberal democratic economies have come to share more in common, as trillions of dollars slosh from one shore to the other. Tourists ply the air routes between New York and Paris. Capitalist institutions, money markets, and registered corporations conduct their businesses throughout the northern and western territorial landmass, moving easily from one country to another.

There is, however, an immediate urgency to closer union of the West. Nearly a half century ago, Henry Kissinger foresaw the need for greater unity of the West. He said: "In the decades ahead, the West will have to lift its sights. When technique becomes exalted over purpose, men become the victims of their complexities. They forget that every great achievement in every field was a vision before it became a reality. Both sides of the Atlantic would do well to keep in mind that there are two kinds of realists: those who use facts and those who create them. The West requires nothing so much as men able to create their own reality."[36]

But as the West grows more unified, it also grows more different from the East. China, a new and rising economy, does not partake of the Western freedom of movement. Capital is not easily mobile into or out of China. Investments have to be negotiated with Chinese firms. Individual Chinese cannot yet invest funds overseas. Chinese exchange rates do not adjust to the movement of capital, or to changes in interest rates. In the Confucian tradition, the state has an all-powerful role in society and people expect it to be supreme. Martin Jacques observes: "It is pointless to think that China is going to change and adopt Western cultural norms: the practices and ways of thinking are simply too old and too deeply rooted for that to happen"[37] China views outside countries as inferior satrapies best suited to a tributary state system. From Beijing's viewpoint, "the European powers have long since exited the region;

their successor power[,] the United States, is now a declining force; and Japan is rapidly being overshadowed by China."[38] China need only wait for the ripe plums of territory and resources to fall into its expanding lap. The insularity and latent hostility of China toward the West is itself a force for Western cohesion.

## Conclusion

The West has been disunited in the past, with European states fighting among themselves. In 1917 and 1941 the American offshoot eventually joined in their balance-of-power wars. But the short-term rise of the Soviet Union after World War II brought only a short-term accommodation among Washington, Paris, and Bonn (later Berlin). When the Soviet Union dissolved in 1991, Western nations went back to business as usual. That did not prevent European unity, which actually increased in the 1990s and 2000s. But the United States temporarily acted as if all problems had been solved. NATO was downgraded, and a rising Asia preoccupied American attention. When the Great Recession struck in 2008, however, it became clear that both sides of the West had to recover in tandem. Banks and investment firms were too closely linked for one to prosper without the other. President Obama encouraged Europe and offered American financial help. Both sides stimulated their economies and neither sought partisan economic advantage: as a result of powerful direct investment in each other, their economic fortunes were tied together. The fate of Bear Stearns or Lehman Brothers was critical to both sides of the Atlantic.

The rise of China cemented the Western connection. Neither could deal with China alone; both had deficits with the

Pacific powerhouse. Both needed Chinese capital. They could regain their footing only by working together. Imperceptibly the social relationships that had brought Europe together after the Second World War were extended across the Atlantic. The trillions invested from one side to the other began to have political effect as individual countries saw their future as linked. These new perceptions emerged as Eastern unity seemed to dissolve. China's rise provoked Eastern countries as well as a newly coordinating West. Japan has allied with it. Increasingly, the West has sought larger economic and political size as an answer to China's growth.

# FOUR

# The Unification of the United States and the Integration of the West

There is a pronounced correlation between rates of economic growth in the United States and its historical acquisition of new territory and resources. The thirteen colonies (states) had a small population of 2–3 million and small territorial assets—less than 400,000 square miles, whose western boundaries were not yet fully defined (figure 3). The Louisiana Purchase in 1803 doubled the size of the existing nation.

By 1850, the thirty-one states had amassed 1.7 million square miles and 23 million citizens. In current dollar terms the GDP had risen from $10 billion in 1790 to $80 billion in 1850. The economy was growing at approximately 30 percent per decade, or 3.3 percent per year. Meanwhile, the American population was increasing rapidly (by a factor of ten), and the U.S. per capita GDP was keeping up with British prosperity, although the British population had risen only by a factor of 2.9. As a consequence, British economic growth during the

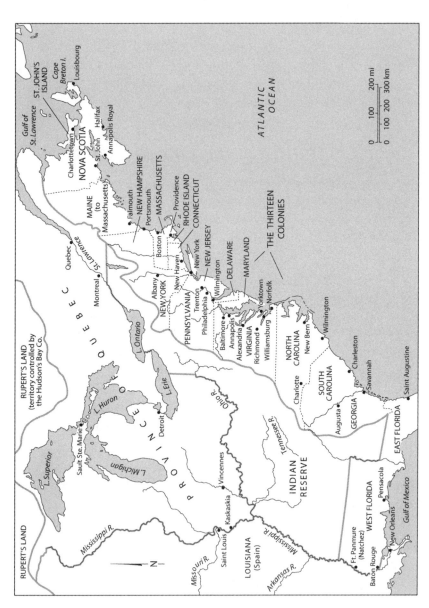

Figure 3. Geographic extent of the thirteen American colonies

same period was between 1 and 2 percent per year less than the American rate.

Other factors also played a role in U.S. development. New infrastructure (canals, roads, and railways) opened up the interior and made settlement possible in the Midwest and Western states. Population increase, including immigration, stoked demand for American products and new innovations like interchangeable parts, textile machinery, and power plants. Toward the end of the nineteenth century, a whole host of new inventions, from the telephone to the electric light bulb, to say nothing of innovations in producing automobiles (the assembly line, for example), made U.S. products both more appealing and less costly than those of competitors. Wages were relatively high, because eastern workers could always choose to go westward to new farms, gold mining, and industrial or service occupations. After 1910 aviation also prospered. But from 1800 to 1870 the opening of new states and territories (including Canada's Klondike in the 1890s) definitely stimulated economic growth in North America.

Just imagine where Americans would be today, if the thirteen colonies had not united and adopted a single currency (initially the continental, and then the U.S. greenback). Suppose there had been tariffs between the colonies, and each had become a fully independent state.[1] Large-scale production would have been stopped, because sales would only be local. With large populations and territories, Texas and California might do well, and perhaps New York, but what would be the market for Delaware goods in, say, Oklahoma? Would these small states achieve any economies of scale for products that had a very limited market? As Barry Eichengreen writes, "Few would doubt that America's prosperity today owes . . .

something to its having been a single market and a monetary union for many decades."[2] The cataclysm of the Civil War fortunately ended in preserving the Union as well as ending slavery, and despite the deep losses on both sides and errant political actions like the Reconstruction era, the Union continued to expand its borders.

Today, including Alaska and Hawaii, the United States covers an area of 3.8 million square miles. Recognizing these realities, one might ask: "should America seek access to another 1.7 million square miles, which is the present size of the European community?" Any such combination would be effective only if it enabled the free flow of capital and goods across the Atlantic, offered a common external tariff, and perhaps made a common currency or a stipulated range of fluctuation among currencies between the two halves of the West. Of course, this would hardly be like settling the Old West in the nineteenth century. Europe is already occupied and has 132 people per square mile (the United States has only 87.4). At the same time, it is worth recalling that Europe's population will be declining from nearly 500 million to 400 million or so in the next forty years. In 2050 the average European's age will be 44.4 years; for Americans, it will be only 40.[3] There will be only two European workers to provide for each retiree, as opposed to four workers now. While Europeans may hesitate how best to make up for this deficit, they may well be attracted by the prospect of new Americans coming to European shores. If one looks at demographic patterns, there are many undersettled regions in southern Europe that as economic conditions warrant might welcome new and industrious workers from America.

The key for both Europe and the United States is to maintain income growth and GDP. No matter how high productivity is, more workers turn out more products. Educational standards in the United States should continue to guarantee that workers remain competent in new skills and technologies. In addition, E.U. accords that ensure labor mobility could facilitate interchanges of talent across the Atlantic bridge. Like American growth, European development has also depended on a continual enlargement of the market and the labor force. The European Customs Union has been trade creating, not trade diverting,[4] and European growth has benefited from the inclusion and integration of new states. How can Europe maintain or increase its position in international hierarchy? One way, of course, is to continue regular admission of Eastern European candidates to its existing number. It seems likely that eight or ten new countries will apply and ultimately be accepted to the European total of twenty-seven, increasing it to thirty-five or more. But no addition to the European community will be as significant as the joining of the United States and Europe in a free trade association.

## The Proposal

What kind of relationship might this be? For the United States and the European Union to join more closely would involve several steps. The first would be fast-track authority for the president to negotiate free trade arrangements without amendments from Congress. Using that authority, the president should initiate proposals for a customs union, leveling tariffs between the two giants. Tariffs are already low, so this step would be important but not have decisive effects. The second step would do away with non-tariff barriers, which currently constitute the most potent barriers to trade: eliminating subsidies, establishing freedom of government contracting for each other, opening up trades and professions, and solving the problem of agriculture, where 40 percent of E.U. euro expenditures now reside. Equally, U.S. farm subsidies that pay farmers not to produce must be changed. This issue cannot be solved in the short term, but a target should be set for open agricultural trade between the two sides of the Atlantic in twenty years. The long-term objective of open markets is mandated by World Trade Organization regulation of customs unions.

Neither continent would then be inundated with grain from the other because costs are high on both sides. Because of the external tariff, the West would remain protected from the most productive Latin American and Australian suppliers. The Common Agricultural Policy (CAP) is scheduled to fall to near 30 percent of the E.U. budget in the next five years. The United States spent $50 billion on farm subsidies in 2010. With mandated budget cuts, this figure will be trimmed by around half over the next ten years. This will occur at the very time when a trade opening to Europe will likely take place.

A customs union will increase trade by a few percentage points; then an agreement to dismantle non-tariff barriers should increase European and American GDP by 0.3–0.5 percent per year;[5] an agreement on a single external tariff would construct barriers against the rest of the world, particularly China.[6] Finally, an agreement limiting currency fluctuation between the two halves of the West would link the dollar and the euro in a common (low-valued) currency stance. This would be particularly important in stimulating Western exports to the rest of the world and increasing Western growth.

## Unification of the United States and Integration of the West

After 1948, the Marshall Plan, NATO, and the demolition of European tariff and currency restrictions raised hopes that Europe and the United States were coming together economically and politically. European investment took place with the proviso that wage increases would not sop up the incentive to new production. U.S. investment moved to Europe in large amounts, buying portions of European businesses.[7] It was reciprocated by European investment and production in the United States during the 1980s and after. Employment and growth increased on both sides of the Atlantic. If, as a consequence, a customs union were created linking Europe and the United States, the longer-term dynamic effects would be marked, favoring growth within the Atlantic union. These might not take place right away. As in early America, political and economic unification would produce long-term rather than short-term growth.

The record U.S. and European growth of 1950–73 was characterized by high investment, low labor costs, and in Europe's case a set of relatively low-valued currencies. This growth was stunted by high oil prices in the 1970s, and afterward by the offshoring of European and American production to Asia. This situation is now changing. Production in China particularly has become more expensive. With productivity gains in both Europe and the United States, in-shoring has become possible for new and also existing plants. The shortening of the workweek in Europe has added to productivity and new investment has followed. It thus becomes very important for a new trade alliance between Europe and America to capitalize on its advantages through home production, high productivity, and the larger markets that would then open. Some proportion of production would still be conducted elsewhere, but the automatic past response of sending all or most new production to China, Thailand, Vietnam, or Bangladesh would change.[8]

## Conclusion

The progressive merger of the economies of Europe and America would lead to the creation of a new and magnetic bloc in world politics, one that would be irresistible to others as well. Japan, Canada, Southeast Asian countries, and eventually China would be drawn into the Atlantic vortex, to their great economic and ultimately political betterment.

# FIVE

# The Trauma of Power Transition

As China rises, will the West come together in time to brush aside the prospect of conflict and possibly war? China is apparently peaceful, but there are many instances in which a rising country has fought with a leading nation. In the historical competition between rising and established powers, either the former leader has acted to derail a rising challenger, or the rising power made an assault on the established leader. Often the domestic politics of one country prompted others to take action. Sometimes a beleaguered leader gained domestic support by acting to put down a foreign threat. Britain entered war with Nazi Germany in September 1939, partly because its people would not allow their leaders to engage in another round of appeasement of Hitler. In other cases authoritarian rulers of a rising state attempted to legitimize their rule by magnifying a foreign conflict.

The shape of an eventual conflict with China depends very

much on when the challenge emerges and which nations take sides. Challengers do not usually act against a strong, cohesive band of allies. But until now a lackadaisical Europe and an America mesmerized by Middle Eastern terrorism did not have a firm grip on the international tiller. They dithered and neglected to steer while China grew strong.

The historical record suggests that rising countries confronting established Western nations pose a significant danger. Ten of the thirteen historical cases of challenge to previously hegemonic countries since the year 1500 have resulted in major war. Only three did not: the United States passed Britain in 1890; the Soviet Union challenged but did not match U.S. economic strength during the Cold War; and Japan passed the Soviet Union economically in 1983. (Of course the Soviet Union was already losing its position as a leading power). The thirteen historical episodes are listed in the notes.[1]

To summarize briefly, rising French kings (Valois) challenged the Hapsburg ascendancy in Italy at the beginning of the sixteenth century. Fifty years later the rising Netherlands sought independence from Spain. As the Dutch were succeeding in the West, Swedish Protestants challenged Austrian Catholics in the Wars of the Reformation in Central Europe.[2] Rising England then took on the Dutch; after an English victory, rising France threw down the gauntlet against England twice, once in the third quarter of the eighteenth century and again in the Napoleonic assault after 1798. In the nineteenth century, Prussia-Germany took on France, and in 1914 Germany attacked England. When America challenged Britain, 1890–1914, British leaders compromised and gave America many of its demands.[3] In the early 1940s Japan and Germany threatened and then attacked the United States, and Germany also went to war with Soviet Russia in 1941. The Soviets did not prevail in their attempt to catch up with the United States in the Cold War. Ultimately in 1989–91, the USSR and the United States ended the Cold War and worked out a rapprochement between them, freeing the previously subject peoples of Communist Eastern Europe.

Hegemony derives from the Greek word "egemonia," whose root is "egemon." This refers to a leader or ruler, often of a state other than one's own. In international relations, "hegemonic powers" strive not only to control subsidiary states but also to provide legitimacy to their leadership, offering values to support it.[4] Some, like Genghis Khan, operated on force alone, smashing resistance. While not neglecting force, British and Dutch rulers devised norms like "rule of law" or "freedom of contract" to legitimize their positions. Challengers thus had to overthrow the normative order as well as its physical dominance to succeed against hegemony. Long-lasting hegemonies endured because of benefits distributed to followers or subordinates, the peripheral countries. Rome, the Dutch Empire, and the British Empire used this technique. Rome's primacy lasted for half a millennium, Britain's for two centuries, and the Dutch for a hundred years. Though challenged, American hegemony began in 1945 and has endured for more than a half century. Some challengers succeeded, but others like France, Germany, and Russia never obtained full international sway. China is about to make its own bid for primacy.

The repetition of war as a consequence of international challenge leads one to ponder the Chinese rise. Will the United States and China come to blows ten years from now or sometime later in the twenty-first century? The most important issue is how to avoid a major war between China and the West in the future.

In all the cases sketched above, no overbalance of power on the side of established major nations existed to dissuade challengers, and a mere balance of potential power was not sufficient to stop a conflict. Hapsburg and Valois kings were evenly balanced, as were French and British competitors. After 1664, the Dutch yielded to British naval power and Britain to American industrial power after 1890. The United States was able to incorporate Japan into its system after 1990 and it will seek to do the same with China. But the United States alone is not strong enough to deter or absorb a Chinese challenge. Washington has only a balance, not an overbalance of power.

In each of the prior historical episodes, the challenger also engaged the hegemonic leader at its weakest or most exposed point, overseas, or on the fringes of its empire. Only Germany, buoyed by memories of the Russian collapse in March 1918, attempted a frontal assault on its eastern neighbor in June 1941. In each case, therefore, the established leader had to consider how important the threat actually was. Could the matter be settled by concession? Did Austria really have to fight over Silesia in 1740? Couldn't Spain be content to keep the southern Netherlands (Belgium), and allow Holland to secede in 1560? How critical was it for France to detach the Hapsburg hold on Italy? In the Thirty Years War (1618–48), the Swedish challenge in Pomerania was not absolutely central to Austria. Challengers sought a weak spot and acted to exploit it. The Second World War started over the German attack on Poland, a nation of little intrinsic interest to either Britain or France. Britain resisted because it could no longer give way to

Germany and remain a Great Power in the eyes of Europe and the world. In sum, challenges to a leading nation can be indirect, or focused on the fringes of power, or they can be direct.

The crucial question is whether such violent transitions can be avoided or dealt with. Avoidance or at least postponement of military challenge depends on the weakening leader associating itself with strong status quo powers.

## World War I as a Test Case

The competition between rising and established powers in the First World War is particularly relevant to the possible conflict between a rising China and the established West. In the First World War there was no overbalance of power on the established side, merely an equal balance on both sides. There were two challengers, Germany and Russia; and two status quo powers, Britain and France (the United States did not join the war until 1917, when Britain's situation became precarious).[5] Beginning in 1897 when Germany built its High Seas Fleet, a move that middle-class Germans overwhelmingly supported, both to rival the British Navy and supposedly to safeguard German trade, the tension between the two countries seemed to escalate relentlessly. British school boys, many of whom later died in horrific battles, used to sing:

In nineteen hundred and ten
the Germans will conquer us then.[6]

But war need not occur with every shift in the relations of power. In the nineteenth century, Otto von Bismarck created an overbalance of power that prevented war for a generation. After Germany's victory in the Franco-Prussian War in 1871, Bismarck began bringing together the key great powers. By

1887, he had developed alignments with Austria, Russia, and England. Only France was left out, a casualty of Germany's seizure of Alsace and Lorraine in 1871. Through this combination, Bismarck had fashioned a peaceful overbalance of power, which restrained both France and Russia.

But following Bismarck's removal from office in 1890, this system began to break down. Bismarck's successors immediately dropped Russia as an ally, and an ordinary balance of power quickly formed in response. France joined with the newly available Russian Empire, and England then came in on the Franco-Russian side. The Triple Entente of France, Russia, and Britain faced the Triple Alliance of Germany, Austria, and Italy, an alignment that led directly to the First World War. Did continental and then world war have to occur?

If Britain had previously linked with Germany and Austria, or if Germany had retained its Russian alliance, there would have been no construction of a Triple Entente to balance the Triple Alliance. Britain would not have formed a connection with France, its primary colonial rival. Instead of balancing alliance systems, there would have been a preponderantly peaceful coalition consisting of Britain and the Triple Alliance grouping.

There has always been the "counterfactual" question whether Germany might have recruited England to substitute for the dropped Russian ally. Bismarck's successor as chancellor, Count Leo Caprivi, favored such an outcome in 1890 and 1891. Joseph Chamberlain sought such a tie in negotiations with Germany between 1899 and 1901.

Germany, however, was interested in acquiring colonies, not from Britain, but from lesser powers like Portugal, Belgium, and Spain. It created the German Navy in 1897 to pressure Britain to permit these acquisitions. This policy succeeded in

1899 when as a result of civil war Germany got Upolu—the main island in Samoa. America obtained the rest. Both Kaiser Wilhelm II and Chancellor Bernhard von Bülow were satisfied that this reinforced their position with German public opinion. But a small island in the South Pacific could not be policed or protected by a fleet considerably inferior to the Royal Navy. The German naval minister Admiral Alfred von Tirpitz needed time to build the High Seas Fleet to the point where England could not risk attacking it without leaving itself vulnerable to a combination of the remaining Great Power navies. This was Tirpitz's so-called "Risk Theory." For this policy to mature, it was important to keep Britain talking until the German High Seas Navy was ready. As Bülow wrote, "in view of our naval inferiority, we must operate so carefully, like the caterpillar before it becomes a butterfly."[7] Though sorely tempted to join, Germany resisted entreaties to form a continental alliance against Britain during Britain's isolated quest to subdue South Africa in the Boer War from 1899 to 1902. But the Risk Theory could not be kept entirely secret if the Reichstag was to vote for further naval increases. Thus Tirpitz had to admit that England was the target of the German naval build-up. Within a very short time, the British people understood German antagonism and began to respond in kind.[8] They also came to recognize that the German Fleet was designed not to protect German commerce on the high seas but to challenge Britain in the North Sea.

The program for German colonial expansion was not the only factor that ruled out a connection with England. Under the machinations of Baron Friedrich von Holstein, the éminence grise of the Foreign Ministry, Germany followed the "Free Hand policy." According to this policy, Germany did not have to associate with England or with Russia, for it deemed that the two wings of Europe—the dual alliance of France and Russia on one hand and splendidly isolated Britain on the other—could never come together. The colonial and naval rivalries between them, Holstein thought, were too great to permit an accord. Therefore Germany had a free hand: it could rebuff England without having to face a Triple Entente of France, Russia, and England.

This belief, of course, turned out to be precisely wrong, and the Triple Entente did eventually form in 1907. From the German point of view in 1900, however, neither Russia and England nor France and England should have been able to get together. Only German pressure and naval building and England's isolation actually made their alliance possible.

Could Germany nevertheless have formed an accord with Britain? It could not if Tirpitz insisted on a navy of forty-five battleships. In persisting, however, Germany lost its central diplomatic and military position in Europe. The British emissary—Lord Haldane—made one final attempt to scale back German naval building in 1912. He did not succeed. German chancellor Theobald von Bethmann Hollweg told him that "public opinion expected a new [naval] law and a third squadron, and he must have these."[9] Negotiations collapsed, and both parties had to consider the possibility of war. Looking back, we can see that the huge German navy was the colossal error of German policy and a mistake that Bismarck would never have made. As long as Germany remained a land power and Britain a sea power, they could agree on a division of spoils and avoid conflict. But once Germany began building a High Seas Fleet in 1897, the basis for compromise disappeared.[10]

Even if Germany could eventually have challenged Britain

economically or politically, it did not need to throw down the gauntlet prematurely. By starting a naval race it could not win, Germany precipitated war (from its aggressive point of view) at the wrong time. It often happens that military preparations lag behind industrial ones. Countries are so impressed with their economic strength that they assume it automatically translates into military superiority. In the First World War, Germany got the worst of both worlds—failure of its territorial ambitions and a costly military defeat besides. Even if they were going to challenge Britain, Germans should have waited until they were ready. Of course, since Britain would win any naval race, this might never have occurred.

An entente with Britain would have served German purposes much better in either event than the ultimately ineffective High Seas Fleet—which brought on conflict, but could not win it. In the 1870s and 1880s, Bismarck pointed to the central German position, and to Berlin as the diplomatic focus of Europe, to convince the legislature and people of Germany's power. But Emperor Wilhelm preferred to exchange diplomatic for military power. If Germany had agreed to Joseph Chamberlain's entreaties in 1899, and an Anglo-German alliance had formed, France and Russia would have remained on the sidelines. France could have pursued its colonial vocations in North Africa only with London's and Berlin's agreement.

## China and the Balance of Power

The balances of power before World War I thus could cause as well as prevent conflict. The flaws of power maneuverings raise the question whether American and Western attempts to rein in China could fail in the twenty-first century. Chinese answers on the ultimate size and uses of its navy are as vague today as the German answers in 1912 when they were refusing to scale down naval preparations. Even the Soviet Union ultimately stopped building nuclear missiles and reached agreement with the United States in the Strategic Arms Limitation Talks (SALT) and the Strategic Arms Reduction Treaty (START). China, however, has agreed to no limit on its arms buildup. It is perhaps making the German mistake.

The pre–World War I balance of power did not prevent war but in essence brought it on. Neither side was definitively deterred from attacking the other. Both sides thought if they acted quickly, they might prevail. Only an overbalance of one central coalition, of the sort that Bismarck formed in 1887, would have prevented conflict in 1914.

Furthermore, it is well to remember that the balance of power does not always form spontaneously, nor does it typically prevent war. An even balance may engender rather than deter war, underscoring an opposition that already exists. Historically, the "balance" frequently does not come together until war is already in the offing; therefore it may reflect an already existing conflict rather than impose any restraint upon it.

A second questionable point is that balance of power theory holds that weaker states will combine to resist the aggressive moves of a stronger state. Why should they do this? If they did not, the power theory argued, the aggressive state would get stronger and more aggressive still. But this fact would not dictate resistance by any particular country. Rather, each individual weak party would have a short-term interest in joining with the aggressor, or at least not drawing his ire. One weak state could not resist a stronger and more aggressive power, and it would seem better to stay on his good side or move to the sidelines.[11] In the early nineteenth century, Napoleon was frequently able to get weaker states to join him before beginning a military encounter with major rivals. The remaining targets of his aggression were then not strong enough to drive him from the field—at least until he made the colossal mistake of invading Russia in 1812.

For a balance of power to form, it must solve what is called the "public goods problem." Briefly, this problem emerges when countries or individuals might collectively benefit from cooperation (to build a road or to resist an aggressor), but each is unsure that others will contribute to obtain the collective good. Accordingly, each holds back—becoming would-be free-riders—and the road or defense pact never materializes. Within a country, government solves the public goods problem by requiring contributions from citizens through taxes. Internationally, however, there is no governmental mechanism to compel cooperation. Some argue that in the long run, weaker states should resist the putative aggressor, but it remains true that each country will do better in the short term by reaching agreement with the larger, stronger state.[12] At the very least, a weak state may buy time by appeasing or "bandwagoning" with the expanding nation. If it decides to issue a military challenge it will be devoured unless others join to protect it, and each of the "protectors" will face public goods costs if they help. It is therefore quite understandable that balances of power have often formed too late to restrain an expanding aggressor. In such cases, the so-called balance of power was not generally a restraint on conflict.[13]

States may find it advantageous to join bigger rather than smaller groups. After World War II, the United States was able to organize a preponderant coalition against Soviet Russia, not a bare balance of power. The Bismarckian alignment bloc in

1887 included Russia, England, and Austria with Germany. Some would claim that this arrangement opened the door for Germany to expand in Europe. In fact, however, Bismarck was balanced not by outsiders but by his own coalition.[14] He could not move in Eastern Europe because of the strong interests there of both Austria and Russia. He could not move west, because Britain would not tolerate another humiliation of France like that of 1871.[15] To the south he would encounter Italy, already an ally. In fact, Bismarck had no urge to move: Germany's secure central position made him a satisfied leader and Germany a satisfied power.

Taking Bismarck's analysis, we should consider the position of China and the United States a decade from today. Right now China is following a policy of gradually undermining the U.S. commitment to the Pacific region. While building up economic ties with Korea and Taiwan, China has now asserted sovereignty over offshore island chains, including the Spratlys, Paracels, Sengakus (Diaoyus), and of course Taiwan and its offshore islands. Japan, South Korea, Brunei, and the Philippines have challenged these claims, but the United States does not know quite how to deal with them. Beijing has not said that it would use military force to acquire these territories, but the islands lie there glimmering as possible victims in the strategic sun. At this point, China does not have the naval power to press its claims to ownership. But it has underscored the theoretical point.[16]

It is perhaps worth remembering that the humiliating Versailles Treaty stripped from Germany areas settled by German populations, in Poland, Czechoslovakia, and elsewhere. Even liberal German governments—ostensibly promising "fulfillment" of the treaty terms, did not willingly acquiesce in ceding German territories to other states. Equally, though France and the Versailles settlement were firmly against it, the idea of uniting Austria and Germany—the two major German nations—also had democratic supporters on the grounds of "national self-determination," which Woodrow Wilson had advocated in the peace talks. The German liberal statesman Gustav Stresemann could do nothing about this militarily. But after 1936 German rearmament allowed Hitler to move to implement it. Because of the theory of national self-determination, neither Britain nor France would stand against the reunification of German territories. This meant that a balance of power against Hitler would be much delayed, if it ever formed at all.

In 1914 there was no overpowering coalition, only a balance that deterred neither side. Britain had paradoxically formed alignment relations ostensibly with its two worst enemies— the colonial rivals France and Russia, both of which sought to punish Germany. France wanted revenge because Germany had seized Alsace-Lorraine in 1871; Russia wanted to stop making unrequited concessions to Austria, a pattern that had started in 1908 with Austria's insistence on annexing Bosnia. By reaching agreement with France and Russia, Britain joined a potentially revisionist coalition that would respond to German and Austrian demarches with unfailing resistance.

If, to the contrary, Britain had been able to fashion an agreement with Germany, the Anglo-German colossus might have stood against all comers. It was prevented only by Germany's "free hand" policy and its insistence on more colonies and a navy to protect them. Such a combination would have left France and Russia with nowhere to go militarily. They could not by themselves have upset the applecart of international relations on the European continent.

The historian Niall Ferguson suggests that if England had delayed sending troops to France in August 1914, it might have undermined French resistance to the German invasion on the Western front. Germany would have outflanked French lines and plowed behind them, capturing Paris. Ferguson believes a moderate peace would then have ensued.[17]

It is true that from 1905 on, German posturing and threatened expansion were a constant problem for other powers. But if Germany had been in league with Great Britain, it might have been less strident, or more successful. Germany would have gained more colonies from cooperating with Britain than it ever could have won through confrontation. Imperial powers frequently helped their allies acquire colonies, as Britain did in Morocco when it assisted France. Germany's prestige and economic growth might have flowered and, thus satisfied, it would not have made war in 1914.

The contemporary situation in the Pacific is very different. There are no majority Chinese countries except Taiwan and Singapore that are not already part of China. But Chinese citizens play important numerical and economic roles in Malaysia, Vietnam, Indonesia, and the Philippines. In Singapore they are the majority, though Malays and Indians also figure importantly in the population. These overseas Chinese can often be counted on to serve mainland economic interests, forging a link with Chinese companies, investment, and production. They are not yet in a position to determine national policy, as the Sudeten Germans were in Czechoslovakia. But they are very influential in local politics and may become more so over time as China becomes an ever larger political, economic, and military factor in the region.

Aside from this, as detailed later, China is progressively

offshoring its final assembly stage of the international production chain to other countries. Instead of fabricating goods in Guangdong or Dalian, China sends them to Malaysia, the Philippines, or Thailand for final and cheaper assembly. Local employment in those countries rises in consequence, and regional governments take notice. Chinese economic influence grows and Western influence declines.

Individual Asian countries are not seduced by Chinese practices. India has few economic ties with Beijing and charts an independent course. It has major boundary disputes with China and needs its connection with the United States. Japan is tempted by China's market but recognizes that Japanese market access depends on transferring high technology to Beijing, which Tokyo is unwilling to do. Territorially, Japan wants the Sengaku Islands because of their oil potential, and is dismayed by China's acceptance of North Korea's military forays against South Korea; Japan sees a Chinese High Seas Fleet as a challenge to the U.S. Seventh Fleet and to its own shipping lanes' access to trade with the rest of world. South Korea is fundamentally anti-Chinese because of Beijing's support of Pyongyang. Hanoi has historically been anti-Chinese and responded strongly when attacked by Chinese armies in 1979. The Philippines, of little account militarily, have territorial disputes with Beijing and have recently offered military facilities to the United States.

Furthermore, acute as the difficulties of the balance of power have been in Europe, they are magnified in East Asia. The Asian nations are even more reluctant solvers of the "public goods problem" than European nations have been. For example, there was no Pacific pact analogous to the Atlantic pact after World War II. Asian powers have not stood up individually or as a group to either Russia or China, but have waited for the United States to take the lead and defend them.

It is thus not clear whether the East Asian powers would autonomously oppose a rising and expanding China in the next ten years. Everything depends on the policy of the United States and Europe; all outcomes require a coherence of the West. A weakening or withdrawing West will not elicit military commitments from any potential balancers in Asia. A retreating United States will only occasion regional parties to adopt a "bandwagoning" response toward China.

Europe and America have yet to create their important rejoinder to such conflicts. That rejoinder is to create the reliable overbalance of power that the international political system needs to deter war. In the past, there were few effective overbalances against a rising challenger. Its creation is by no means a foregone conclusion. Perhaps Japan will join the West not long after the West unites, but can the United States count on any arrangement that is more powerful than that which existed in 1914? As China's economic power grows, it could seek to counter the West by an alliance with Moscow.

## Avoiding a New World War I

World War I—and the counterfactual possibility of avoiding it through a British-German understanding—raises questions about how the West should deal with China today. Europe and America have yet to create a credible overbalance of power that the international political system needs to deter war. To accomplish this, the two halves of the West—the European Union and the United States of America—must come together economically and politically. Drawing in Japan as well,

Figure 4. Map of Eurasia
(Maxx-Studio/Shutterstock)

the West would construct a system that was impervious to challenge.

What then? One shibboleth of international relations theory is that China would take an ally to counterbalance what would appear to be a superior Western combination. The presence of the Shanghai Cooperation Organization (which includes Russia, China, Tajikistan, Uzbekistan, Kyrgyzstan, and Kazakhstan) makes Russia a plausible candidate. The logic of geopolitics might support this choice. All geographers understand that the dominant land mass in world politics is the World Island of Eurasia (figure 4). In Eurasia, population, resources, and technology cluster together. If a single coalition controlled the entire World Island, from Calais to the Kamchatka Peninsula, no other grouping could stand against it. That cannot happen so long as the West coheres.

A Russian-Chinese combination is exceedingly unlikely. The two nations have never been friends: they are rivals in Asia, and that rivalry may increase. It is much more likely that China would ultimately join the West—which it is industrially wedded to in any event. This would then create an "agglomeration" in world politics that would obviate any need for balance. As we shall see later, it is much more efficient to draw a potential aggressor into one's coalition than to oppose him. Perhaps Germany could have been drawn in by England, but only if a less volatile kaiser had rejected naval building and the Free Hand theory. Though it may not yet realize it, China remains the ultimate suitor of the West.

## Conclusion

The problem that arises when one big state or center of power passes, or threatens to pass, a hegemonic leader was first formulated by Thucydides. The Peloponnesian Wars were one result of such an occurrence, and World War I was another. Soon China will pass the United States of America, and the world wonders whether the result will be another gigantic military conflict. Yet the world has always had another string to its bow—the possibility of agglomerating power and peacefully bringing the rising state into an established central coalition. This possibility sets the stage for the rest of this book.

# SIX

# Market Clusters Augment Size

Rising and declining major powers may come to blows as both maneuver to obtain greater political and economic size, the dominant objective of modern states. But it is also possible that the international marketplace could help draw the West—the United States and Europe—closer to China, just as such trends have previously linked Japan and the West. This chapter argues that economic factors can bring China and the West closer, making war less likely.

How will this happen? America and the West achieve bigness by a greater agglomeration of the two economies. This would attract, not alienate, Beijing. As the United States and Europe capture industries based on economies of scale, they grow larger and their market becomes more attractive internationally. The reverse is also true: the larger the home market, the greater the likelihood that economies-of-scale industries will concentrate there. With an E.U. population of 500 million, European industries have very large markets within the union even if they do not sell abroad. Likewise, American corporations cut their teeth on the home market of 300 million people and then examine possibilities overseas. Japan's do likewise. Overseas production chains emerge when the lower links in the manufacturing process can be done more cheaply elsewhere. In the past, and to some degree today, Germany, Japan, and the United States have created production chains to overcome some of the restraints on trade that would otherwise prevent sales abroad. China will accept imported components if these can be bundled into new products that Beijing can turn around and ship back to the West.

Greater production erects new citadels of industrial power in Europe, the United States, and Japan. Economies-of-scale industries cluster in particular locations. China is attracted by these and develops ties with them. Particularly fruitful sites draw in other industries and skilled labor to their favored places. Computer products, microprocessors, and software migrate to Silicon Valley on the West Coast. Health products, pharmaceuticals, and biotechnology center in Boston, Cambridge, and their environs. Fashion goes to Milan and Paris. This does not mean that these industries could not be established elsewhere, in Guangdong, for example, or Taiwan. But it does suggest that economies of scale will be concentrated regionally.

## Regionalism of Scale Versus the Spread of Industry

Some commentators now assert that "the world is flat." *New York Times* columnist Tom Friedman has convinced many that the East is equalizing the West's previous advantage and sooner or later all economic regions will become the same—the capital and technology of one region will uniformly spread to others. According to this view, the migration of economic skills, capital, and labor would ultimately mean that Silicon Valley will have no greater power of attraction than, for example, Namibia as a location for economic activity. Friedman is certainly right in saying that the East is rising. It is also true that labor skills, educational attainment, and capital are spreading to other locations. The question is whether the New East will be fully independent from the Old West in its command of technology and industrial power.

Many countries have sought technological independence but not achieved it. Cutting off trade with the West, Josef Stalin thought the Soviet Union could become totally self-sufficient in the 1930s and after. But he did not achieve economic independence, and his efforts to do so stunted Soviet development. The nation lost access to the best technology developed in democratic states. Though its heavy industry marched ahead in the 1950s and 1960s, it did so by copying outmoded Western designs and processes, and the economic system was disastrously inefficient. The Soviet Union did not keep pace with the progress of Western technology. In a contrasting example, Japan grew at 10 percent a year in the 1960s, and 4 percent in the 1980s, by maintaining its links with and exploiting Western technology. It is true that after 1987, Japan's capitalism did not sustain its high growth, but this was because of the satisfaction of its middle class with the wealth already achieved. When Japan resumed growing after the year 2000, it not only kept the economic links that bound it to the West and the United States, it intensified them. In more general terms, if Eastern nations want to keep up with the progress of technology, they similarly need to be connected to Western economies.

This is so because potent centers of economic dynamism tend to remain in place. Economies of scale give an advantage to large firms in large states; costs per unit decline as the number of units produced increases, and firms with access to large markets are better able to exploit these economies. Up to now, economies of scale have been limited to the West and Japan. China, Korea, and Vietnam benefit because they associate with Western firms and form links in the production chains that sell in Western markets. South Korea's Samsung and Hyundai have also achieved scale effects but link themselves with Western and Japanese firms. They would not ultimately prosper if they did not continue and enhance these ties.

## Distance Lends Disenchantment

Taken to an extreme, a "flat world" suggests the "death of distance." Transport costs are low; communication costs lower still. The pervasive adoption of Skype means that visual contact is never lost. Have we achieved a homogeneous universe in which anything can be based anywhere without extra cost? Not really. The persuasive finding that dictates the future of the world's industry is not the irrelevance of distance but the triumph of place. By "place," I do not mean some particular place, but rather that geographic closeness, similar institutions, languages, cultures, and educational attainment are now much more important than the economist's "transport costs" in dictating economic success. Transport and communications costs can continue to decline without leveling cultural and technological barriers. Once economies-of-scale industries cluster in a particular location, other allied firms and labor supplies are likely to go there as well. This is as true of Bangalore and Toyota City as it is of Silicon Valley and Route 128 in Boston.

Thus regions that can cluster together because of their social similarities have an intrinsic and lasting advantage. Tobler's Law, that "everything is related to everything else but near things are more related than distant things," remains true.[1] The data show that a 1 percent increase in geographic distance leads to a 1 percent decrease in trade between countries. Two countries with a common language trade 42 percent more than similar countries that speak different languages. Countries trade with fellow members of a trade bloc 47 percent more than they trade with similar countries outside their trade bloc. This amount is increased by 114 percent if the two countries share a common currency. If these countries were once part of the same colonial administration, they trade with each other 188 percent more than countries lacking that prior association. Adjoining countries carry on 125 percent more trade than nations with no common border. Geography and culture ultimately dictate the degree of economic closeness, and this closeness undergirds success.[2] It is true that Europe and North America are three thousand miles apart, but America and China are six thousand miles from each other. This does not mean that production chains will not bring devices to the Western consumer from assembly plants in Thailand or China. Nor does it suggest that Starbucks or McDonald's will not cater to customers in Beijing. Rather, it argues that the production chains of previously established economies-of-scale industries will govern or strongly influence what each region does.[3]

## Karl Deutsch and Globalization

Some of the major questions that confront us today were anticipated by Karl Deutsch, the Harvard scholar who first charted the trends of nationalism and social integration a half century ago. He concluded that a flat world will never emerge. Flatness is not determined simply by transport costs declining to very low levels, or Internet communications costs falling to zero. The closeness of countries and cities—and also their economic relationships—are determined by values, institutions, common or different languages, migration, and historical usages. For practical purposes these cultural and political traits will never be homogenized into one culture, one language, or one set of values.[4] If that did happen, the world would become one country—which it certainly is not yet doing.

Writing in the 1950s and 1960s, Deutsch saw some countries moving so close to others that peaceful change between them could be counted on to endure. He listed three cases where peace had already arrived: between Norway and Sweden; Canada and the United States; and Belgium, the Netherlands, and Luxembourg. In each instance, the identity of values, cultures, institutions, and the mutual comprehension of different languages meant the end of war. The intensity of messages (including immigration and tourism) going back and forth led each country to feel a part of the other, generating a close approximation to neighborliness and fellow-feeling. They had overcome a past history in which Belgium revolted from Holland; both had been occupied by Napoleonic France, and Luxembourg had been part of Austria, Holland, and Germany.

This did not mean that nationality was a constant. Newcomers entering the social scene could change political attitudes. For a time Finland felt comfortable being ruled by Sweden. But when its latent rural population was mobilized to activity through growth in literacy and political participation,

Finnish nationality bubbled to the surface. The same was true of Czech national consciousness under the German-speaking Austrian Empire. The core of Czech nationalism was born in the revolutions of 1848, which mobilized the population of Bohemia to political activity against its Austrian rulers.

Just as the intensity of internal messages could lead a population to assert itself, if transactions and messages with the outside world outweighed purely domestic messages, nationality could break down. The independence movements directed against Soviet rule of Eastern Europe throughout the 1980s finally penetrated Soviet Russia in 1991, and its borders were reshaped accordingly. Globalization represents such a set of messages, and in theory it might undermine nationality. If so, Friedman could be right. In fact, however, the major finding of recent research is precisely the opposite. Instead of homogeneous leveling of all states on one great plain, states seem to have formed into strong clusters, erecting a new hill above the plain. The E.U., NAFTA (the North American Free Trade Area), and its South American equivalent, Mercosur, have brought these regional neighbors closer together.

Europe has continued to integrate, and the "pluralistic security community" that once embraced Scandinavia and the Benelux nations has now been extended to France and Germany. As other nations adopt the *acquis communautaire*—the common agreement—of the European Union, erstwhile enemies like Croatia and Serbia will lay down their arms against each other, and Bosnia will join them.

## Economies of Scale

Paul Krugman, Brian Arthur, and Allen Scott carry Deutsch's argument even further, positing the development of agglomeration effects where certain industries become dominated by a few large firms.[5] Some industries achieve these economies on a worldwide basis: civilian aircraft, software, microprocessors, finance, conventional arms industries, auto producers, insurance, and increasingly cinema-entertainment each have fewer than ten world-class firms. At this point China has no such industries, though it participates in production chains with several of them.[6]

Once an area achieves economies of scale, regionally linked industries and their associated cities strengthen ties through gravity effects and come still closer together. Where industries are big and geographically linked, the development of one industrial complex stimulates the development of another. Look at the East Coast of North America, from Boston to North Carolina, or Silicon Valley with its technological tendrils stretching from Seattle to San Diego. Initially Silicon Valley centered on Stanford and San Jose, then broadened north and south. New York's financial industry widened to include Charlotte, North Carolina. Boston's expertise in pharmaceuticals and health products extended southward to New Jersey and Pennsylvania. When industries concentrate in particular locales, sophisticated technicians congregate nearby to gain job flexibility and greater opportunity. Companies in turn concentrate there to gain access to the most talented workers. The process is self-reinforcing.

A uniform distribution of technical competencies throughout the planet (the flat world) would undermine the economies of scale that are generated by rising clusters of information located in particular places. The world has not become flat. Instead, the hills and valleys created by the clustering of expertise and employment will always be with us. Gravity effects operate both inside and outside a state. Inside, they bring industries together in geographic clusters. Outside, they dictate that the growth of large states will affect neighboring economies. Within states, large cities and associated labor forces remain linked as an economic dynamo. At the moment there are between twenty and forty urban areas on a worldwide basis that stimulate and house new industries (figure 5).

Eight of these are in Asia, three in Latin America, thirteen in Western Europe, and another seven in North America.[7] These regional spark plugs seek to achieve economies of scale—a lowering cost curve that attracts new industry to their locations.[8] Though large in population, Shanghai, Shenzhen, and Beijing have yet to achieve this industrial standard.

The Harvard economist Edward Glaeser contends that "our species learns primarily from the aural, visual, and olfactory clues given off by our fellow humans," which in turn require the physical presence of individuals.[9] "The Internet," writes Glaeser, "is a wonderful tool, but it works best when combined with knowledge gained face-to-face, as the concentrations of Internet entrepreneurs in Bangalore and Silicon Valley would attest." "The declining cost of connecting over long distances has only increased the returns to clustering close together." He adds: "since new technologies have increased the returns from new ideas, they have also increased the returns from face to face collaboration."[10] The barriers affecting trade are not simply distance or transport cost. True economic closeness requires trust and understanding between countries and regions. Anthony Venables writes: "Face-to-face contact enables higher frequency interchange of ideas than is possible by e-mail, phone or video-conference. Brainstorming is hard to do without the ability to interrupt and use parallel means

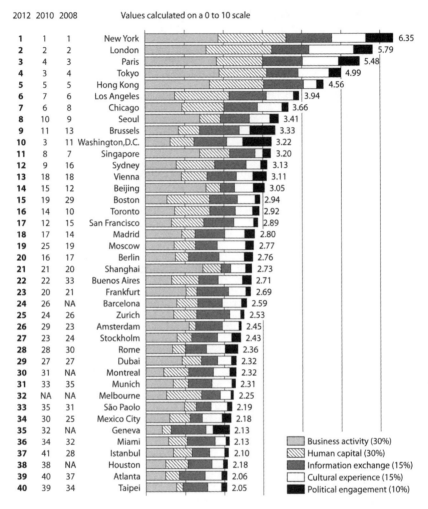

| 2012 | 2010 | 2008 | | Values calculated on a 0 to 10 scale | |
|---|---|---|---|---|---|
| 1 | 1 | 1 | New York | | 6.35 |
| 2 | 2 | 2 | London | | 5.79 |
| 3 | 4 | 3 | Paris | | 5.48 |
| 4 | 3 | 4 | Tokyo | | 4.99 |
| 5 | 5 | 5 | Hong Kong | | 4.56 |
| 6 | 7 | 6 | Los Angeles | | 3.94 |
| 7 | 6 | 8 | Chicago | | 3.66 |
| 8 | 10 | 9 | Seoul | | 3.41 |
| 9 | 11 | 13 | Brussels | | 3.33 |
| 10 | 3 | 11 | Washington,D.C. | | 3.22 |
| 11 | 8 | 7 | Singapore | | 3.20 |
| 12 | 9 | 16 | Sydney | | 3.13 |
| 13 | 18 | 18 | Vienna | | 3.11 |
| 14 | 15 | 12 | Beijing | | 3.05 |
| 15 | 19 | 29 | Boston | | 2.94 |
| 16 | 14 | 10 | Toronto | | 2.92 |
| 17 | 12 | 15 | San Francisco | | 2.89 |
| 18 | 17 | 14 | Madrid | | 2.80 |
| 19 | 25 | 19 | Moscow | | 2.77 |
| 20 | 16 | 17 | Berlin | | 2.76 |
| 21 | 21 | 20 | Shanghai | | 2.73 |
| 22 | 22 | 33 | Buenos Aires | | 2.71 |
| 23 | 20 | 21 | Frankfurt | | 2.69 |
| 24 | 26 | NA | Barcelona | | 2.59 |
| 25 | 24 | 26 | Zurich | | 2.53 |
| 26 | 29 | 23 | Amsterdam | | 2.45 |
| 27 | 23 | 24 | Stockholm | | 2.43 |
| 28 | 28 | 30 | Rome | | 2.36 |
| 29 | 27 | 27 | Dubai | | 2.32 |
| 30 | 31 | NA | Montreal | | 2.32 |
| 31 | 33 | 35 | Munich | | 2.31 |
| 32 | NA | NA | Melbourne | | 2.25 |
| 33 | 35 | 31 | São Paolo | | 2.19 |
| 34 | 30 | 25 | Mexico City | | 2.18 |
| 35 | 32 | NA | Geneva | | 2.13 |
| 36 | 34 | 32 | Miami | | 2.13 |
| 37 | 41 | 28 | Istanbul | | 2.10 |
| 38 | 38 | NA | Houston | | 2.18 |
| 39 | 40 | 37 | Atlanta | | 2.06 |
| 40 | 39 | 34 | Taipei | | 2.05 |

Business activity (30%)
Human capital (30%)
Information exchange (15%)
Cultural experience (15%)
Political engagement (10%)

Figure 5. Great metropolitan cities of the world. The chart lists the
world's most economically powerful cities in order of their scores on a
combined measurement of global influence across five dimensions: business
activity, human capital, information exchange, cultural experience,
and political engagement.
(Adapted by Bill Nelson from A.T. Kearney Global Cities Index,
copyright A.T. Kearney, 2012, all rights reserved, adjusted and
reprinted with permission)

of communication—oral, visual, and body language. Face-to-face is also important for building trust."[11] When Hollywood producers are planning a new venture they can set it up over the phone, but they need to meet to finalize the arrangements. In these negotiations body language is everything.

Industrial concentration is made possible by urban density. Specialist manufacturing or niche consumer items (like hand-tooled boots, mobile pet grooming, Eurasian cuisine, or artisanal coffee) require large numbers of specialist users in one place. London's Jermyn Street, Savile Row, and the City of London, America's Silicon Valley, and Los Angeles' movie industry, concentrate clients and producers near one another. As these regions consolidate, living costs rise and housing prices may move upward. Dense urban neighborhoods need high-rise apartments to supply the demand. Land is too expensive for ranch homes with croquet lawns in Manhattan and it is becoming so in Beverly Hills.

Talent may gravitate to densely settled locations to enhance interaction. At UCLA, economist Edward Leamer points out that economies of scale can operate when there are no cultural incentives in a particular place. He asks: "Suppose there were no spatial-ethnic barriers or transport costs within the United States, how many Hollywoods would there be?" His answer: "still—'only one.'" The key point is that we are witnessing an increasing regionalization of globalization. It is an admixture that means greater intensive globalization in some parts of the world than in others. What is true in Hollywood is also true in India. Even without internal cultural differences, there would be only one Bollywood, and it would still be located in Mumbai, not Calcutta (now Kolkata). Globalization works where regional economies of scale are concentrated. It fails if large firms cannot achieve a declining cost curve. Around the world, some industries achieve economies of scale and others do not. So far, China has no economies-of-scale industries. The economist Shujie Yao writes: "To meet its ambitions and become a rich and powerful nation [China] will require [its] multinationals to flourish overseas. But without its own respected brands, its Toyotas and Samsungs, China will always languish at the lower end of the value chain."[12]

In contrast to the paucity of industrial concentrations in many Asian countries, Europe and America have many economies-of-scale firms in aircraft, software, hardware, luxury goods, entertainment, chemicals, pharmaceuticals, automotive firms, insurance, and finance. A full uniting of the West would extend the existing globalization regionally. Common language, common culture, common institutions, and common democratic traditions would heighten economic linkages and provide for an integration that would further stimulate growth on both sides of the Atlantic bridge.

If the European Union and Canada–United States form a closer customs arrangement, tariff barriers outside and non-tariff easements within would make it less necessary to export outside this union. As of 2004, the European Union held 39 percent of its total foreign direct investment in North America, its highest on any continent. In 2007 the United States held 48 percent of its foreign direct investment in the European Union. A further trade agreement between the two would lead to an estimated $120 billion increase in trade and $180 billion increase in growth over the next five years.[13] Given these figures, one would worry less about the trade balance with China and East Asia. China would sell less abroad and more to itself, but it would still be investing in production chains that make exporting possible, thereby tying China in to the Western marketplace. As reports in the *Financial Times* suggest, China would be trying to acquire high technology to make its investment in Western firms profitable, as the Chinese company Geely has sought to do with Volvo.[14]

## States and Firms

Today, all major industrial countries depend on markets and raw materials located elsewhere. None of them except possibly Russia is fully self-sufficient in raw materials. And Russia lags in every area but raw materials. With this omnipresent need for materials or resources, how do countries manage their interdependence with others?

In the first place, economic development stems from trade. At some point China will be rich enough to develop through the consumption purchases of its 1.3 billion people. Until then, its growth will depend on selling abroad, and even afterward China will still need foreign exchange to purchase the oil and minerals that it lacks at home. China is more dependent on foreign oil and natural gas than the United States. Like firms, countries are interdependent. Firms compete, rise, and decline: facing difficulties, they merge with others to find new economies. States are similar; their long-term position depends upon generating wealth and achieving economic growth, which requires selling abroad. States acquire production in other countries to avoid tariffs on their goods. They invest abroad to raise their returns. A globalized world involves the movement of factors of production among different states. Acquiring or losing those factors is of great importance to national decision-makers. Their presence or absence means national employment or economic diminution. If a country loses factors to other nations, as Spain did to Holland in 1600, as Holland did to England after 1650, or as Britain did to the United States after 1920, governments lose power and national unity is shaken. The problem the West faces in the longer term is how to control the key factors of production—capital, technology, and labor—and keep them at home. It still seems to have control of the most important elements of those factors—skilled labor, capital, and technology. But it will not retain them if the Western market is not enlarged and demand increased. Factors always flow to where the returns are highest.

States and firms are different in many ways. Countries are supposedly democratically controlled or at least influenced by their peoples, but firms have few obligations other than to their stockholders. While companies specialize in particular products, states are not expected to engage in a division of labor among their number. Yet firms create a division of labor when they outsource production to companies overseas.

States also depend on markets, raw materials, and technology located in other nations. Companies have become flatter, in that they do fewer things in-house, contracting many of their previous activities out to others. Countries are also flatter, in that they deal with other states for vital services. Industrial alliances, international production arrangements, and subcontracting of component production all make the classical theory of international politics, which posits that states are "like units," less and less relevant to modern politics. They are increasingly "unlike units." Some countries like Australia and Russia produce raw materials; some do intermediate components, like Taiwan, Singapore, Hong Kong, and Bangladesh. Others do final assembly, like China, Korea, Mexico, and Poland. Some nations design products, find markets, finance their production, and oversee the entire process, like Europe, the United States, and Japan.

Perhaps two-thirds of the production on which modern industrialized states depend takes place in other countries. In its efforts to increase its economies of scale in production, the United States cannot get along without Japanese, Mexican, and Canadian industry. One country sends foreign direct investment into another country. Dependent on that production, it will encounter difficulties if that source is cut off. Finding another production unit will be a complicated and lengthy affair. If Foxconn—the giant component producer in China— is not available, how will Apple find a substitute?

Dependence is reinforced if the investing country does not possess similar capabilities at home. Earthquakes or typhoons in Taiwan can affect the world's access to flat panel screens. The tsunami in Japan temporarily cut off Western producers from key Japanese-designed goods. Floods in Thailand shut down auto component production for Japan. In finance the dependence may even be more acute. Greece and Portugal may be dependent on German or American capital to buy their bonds. There may be no alternative purchasers (except the European Central Bank). In 1927–29 when bonds of the Weimar Republic were coming due, Americans did not refinance them, and there were no alternative buyers. As a result, Germany could not pay its reparations bills. To sell its bonds, Berlin was forced to raise interest rates, sending the country into a deep depression. This decline paved the way for Hitler's accession to power on January 30, 1933.

More generally, for some efficient industries, the long-term cost curve may decrease with increased production. Outsourcing allows a firm to produce at a lower unit cost. Ultimately, however, a firm's production of a particular item may reach a practical limit, or the returns on that particular product may decrease. The new razor may be outmoded by a competitor's razor with four or five blades. The firm may want to diversify out of razors and into, for example, cutlery, hairdryers, or bicycles—or smart phones, tablets, or other gadgets. The firm may seek new technology from merger with a small producer. It may seek new markets abroad. In any event the producer facing a disadvantage in sales of a given product will try to broaden or diversify its product offerings. Frequently this will mean a merger with foreign firms or production arranged to regain market share, as Procter and Gamble did in buying Gillette some years ago.

States face similar incentives. Confronting rising tariffs after 1880, England could no longer sell most of its wares in continental Europe.[15] It had to find other markets for them, and did so by renewing the quest for colonial territories as markets. Empire is not a solution today, but customs unions with other large entities form an important part of a solution. This suggests that states need connection with other states in the same way that businesses need connection with other firms. States, like businesses, need new synergies or new products. To regain market power and find new demand for its products, a country may need to merge with another nation.

A corporation does not have to please an internal clientele. A state, however, needs to make sure that its economic decisions meet the political needs and demands of its citizenry. A corporation does not hesitate when it is setting up cheaper production abroad. Shareholders will not object. But if a country that has shunted much of its production to overseas suppliers finds that it has lost jobs at home, it cannot lay off citizens. Therefore a country has two masters: the demands of the international market, and the demands of its own political system. To serve one may be to frustrate the other. This is why American teenagers are learning French and Chinese, and their foreign counterparts English.

American industry, represented, for example, by General Electric, has no hesitancy outsourcing jobs in order to reduce costs. But the United States wishes to keep those jobs at home. On the other hand, if U.S. corporations fail, the country ultimately fails with them. Its technological preeminence rests on research and development undertaken by American corporations. They must be allowed to operate overseas and to manufacture overseas or they will go out of business. America, Japan, and Germany have striven to solve this problem in different ways. Since the mid-1990s Japan has been in the doldrums economically. Its international corporations continue to export high-technology products overseas, but domestic demand has been too small to sustain its half of Japanese industry. The Japanese rate of growth has fallen. Japan has succeeded internationally by employing foreign labor, providing Chinese province chiefs or U.S. governors with efficient new factories.

The United States erred by investing too much in finance, which created esoteric products like credit default swaps, whose arcane manipulation brought the collapse of AIG in 2008. Hedge funds and even Goldman Sachs benefited by selling their clients key financial instruments and then shorting them (that is, financially betting on their decline). The net financial contribution to the U.S. physical stock of capital was negligible. Taking this into account, many American college graduates have turned their backs on finance and moved to companies that actually create something of value. Germany, conversely (with international assistance), made physical products—cars, pharmaceuticals, and health care products that could be sold abroad without loss of employment at home. Germany reduced labor costs by picking up some of the health care costs and changing apprenticeship requirements. Industrious German labor could actually produce the same amount with fewer hours of work.

This last advantage is relevant for the United States. Labor costs go down when productivity (output per labor hour) goes up. Increases in productivity then can keep highly productive labor employed and reduce the outsourcing of jobs. The key to success is the amount of value added. If low-value-added jobs are shipped overseas, this will not affect highly skilled employment at home. The key for both Germany and the United States is to retain jobs at the high end of the value spectrum. Then it becomes possible to export the assembly of high-tech goods overseas without losing domestic employment. To do this, both Germany and the United States have to assist research and development expenditures so that industry stays ahead of the curve of international competition. Neither will fill some links of the supply chain as cheaply as China or Vietnam does. But the key is to keep the higher links at home. To do this, the work force must be highly educated and trained for specialist niches in the production process. The engineering of the workplace must be not only understood but also advanced by worker-specialists.

This leads to our present understanding of economic interdependence. It is not enough to export abroad and achieve an export surplus or at least a balance. Everything depends upon what one exports and what elements in the production chain one controls.

## Interdependence and Production Chains

No major industrial country now accounts for all aspects of any major manufactured product. They may design and market it or do the research and development. They may finance the production process. They may manufacture some or most of the components or assemble those components into the final consumer good. The ultimate price of the good reflects the contributions made at each stage of the production process. Western companies may design the product and provide the computer chips that control its operation. But manufacture of components and their assembly into a neat bundle is left to others. Typically, the component manufacturer and the assembler together earn less than 50 percent of the product's retail price.

Accordingly, though Chinese manufacture will be included in the final price of the good, China will typically receive only 30 or so percent of that price. So, for example, Chinese exports of $500 billion do not mean that China actually received the full one half trillion dollars, but rather something like $150 billion. Therefore an important part of the Chinese balance-of-trade surplus with the United States and Germany, for example, may largely represent earnings by American or German corporations. The import content of China's exports is very high. The need to be part of Western (and Japanese) production chains links China and other countries with Western nations.

Outsourcing means that one country after another joins

the production chain. The most globalized societies are heavily linked through production chains with other suppliers. In the words of Stephen Brooks, "the globalization of production has shifted the scales against great power revisionism" (that is, military expansion).[16] If an aggressor conquers another country, for example, it will find it has gained only part of the production chain. If it gets the top end—design, research and development, and marketing skills, the aggressor will not be able actually to consume its victim's goods without finding other countries with component manufacturers and assemblers to complete the product. This may be difficult to do. Suppose, for example, Russia conquered Europe. The Kremlin would not gain access to Europe's sophisticated stock of consumer goods, because it would not possess the suppliers that rendered designs and components into a finished product. Alternatively, imagine that India conquered China. Delhi would then possess final assembly and components, but it would not get design, R&D, and computer technology—it would have to buy these from someone else or develop them on its own. It is not by any means clear that outsiders would be willing to provide such items. In consequence, aggression for the purpose of achieving mastery of the full range of industrial processes may well be a vain proposition.

In addition, aggression would cut the links vital to maintain exports. Export-led development in Asia means selling in Western and Japanese markets. (Developing markets in the Far East cannot presently absorb the range of products that are now purveyed to the United States and Europe.) One basic restraint on war between the United States and China is China's need to sell the goods it has assembled to Europe or the United States. Attacking either Europe or America would

|  | China | Germany |
|---|---|---|
| Total exports | 27.4% | 27.2% |
| Total manufactures | 30.4% | 30.9% |
| Low/medium-low-tech manufactures | 21.6% | 33.2% |
| High/medium-high-tech manufactures | 37.5% | 27.8% |
| Information communications technology (ICT) manufactures | 48.5% | 29.0% |

*Source:* OECD Structural Analysis (STAN) Input-Output Database, Imports content of exports as % of GDP

set back China's growth. China cannot yet develop solely by selling consumption goods to its own population.

Germany and China both export goods with a high import content. The difference between them is that the import content in German goods is largely low tech in character, including components or raw materials (Germany adds the high-tech content). In China's case the import content is largely high- and medium-tech goods—small computers, sensing devices, and electronics. (China adds the lower-tech content.) China would not be able to export effectively if the final goods it assembles did not contain this key foreign content. China, which cannot contribute this content itself, thus receives only about 30 percent of the value added for the product as a whole. Germany includes low-tech (imported) content in its exported goods, but derives 60 percent of the value added. Germany could provide those components or assembly by itself if it chose to, but it contracts them out for cost reasons, not because it cannot make them at home.

What does this difference mean for international politics? It suggests that developing countries do not easily emancipate themselves from the discipline of the international market. To be saleable in Western markets, their goods must embody sophisticated content provided by others. China's growth is thus interdependent growth. In this way it is unlike German growth in the late nineteenth century, which was also based on international trade. But Germany did not then participate in production chains in which most of the value-added content was provided by others. It provided that content. Germany was therefore not as dependent for its own national progress on the international system as China is today.

The world's industrial structure has brought East and West closer than ever before. Development has been determined by integral relationships between Eastern and Western capitalism that despite the vicissitudes of international relations are likely to endure. But the key question is whether China and other rising states will strive to emancipate themselves from and substitute for the central connections that have governed and stimulated their rise up to now. Russia, a late industrializer, was deeply entangled in the network of capitalist interdependence during the nineteenth century. Even after the Bolshevik Revolution, Russia remained tied to capitalist markets and technology during the New Economic Policy period of 1921–28. But after 1933, Communist Russia resolved to go it alone, cutting its industrial links with the West. Will China act similarly in the years to come?

## Conclusion

This chapter has shown that countries benefit from economies-of-scale industries, which make for much larger production runs. Rising countries will wish to have connections with such industries in order to participate in their production chains and sell goods abroad. China particularly has done so. At the same time, there has been no major transfer of market clusters to the developing world. These have remained in the West and its industrial associate, Japan, creating strong links between regions that did not exist in previous history. There were no "production chains" in 1914. The world's economic interdependence today stitches manufacturing places together. If they do not stay linked, any country that opts out will suffer in economic growth and technological capability.

There are however, temptations of flatness that might lead new nations to believe they can duplicate or dispense with previous industrial interdependence. One might be led to think that economies-of-scale industries would suddenly sprout up all over. To a sufficiently enterprising technician in information technology, it might seem that everything can take place in a home or computer garage. Three-dimensional printing makes possible the use of sand, epoxy, and composites in a wide variety of locations. If they could be fully exploited, scale would not be necessary, and (at the theoretical limit) one could design and produce anywhere.

In fact, however, place still dominates. Talented and skilled workers congregate together. Economies of scale still exist for quantity production of a product. These efficient industries are located in the West and Japan. China will need to draw near these powerful market clusters to maintain its growth and productivity.

# SEVEN

# The Problem of China

China is the most dependent of the great powers. It has little oil, iron, or raw materials. It does not yet have indigenous capability in high technology but largely derives its industrial processes from Western and Japanese innovation. Besides industrial design, the things China needs are generally not available in its own neighborhood. Great sources of oil exist in the Middle East, six thousand miles from Chinese ports. Other raw materials like iron ore are located in Australia and Brazil, again thousands of miles away. Trade is therefore essential to Chinese security and economic welfare, and it does not appear that military aggression to seize new raw-materials areas would be practical because of distance. The likelihood of opposition leaves China with little prospect of building the most powerful navy or the most powerful air or missile force in the world.

But history suggests that rising nations partly disregard

their interdependence with great powers and other countries. In the heady flush of rapid advance, modernizing countries chafe at restrictions. The United States did so in the nineteenth century when it seized or bought continental territory from its neighbors. Some historians have called America a "dangerous nation" as it moved relentlessly westward. Russian development was similar. Russian explorers and some settlers reached the Pacific at the end of the seventeenth century. With most of their territory closer to the North Pole than the equator, Russians wanted a warmwater port, and tried but failed to get Constantinople, the Black Sea gateway to the Mediterranean. As the Turkish Empire weakened in the nineteenth century, Russia tried to expand into the former Turkish territories in the Balkans. Again, it did not succeed. Massive Russian railway building, however, brought West European territory within Russia's military reach at the beginning of the twentieth century.

China might feel similar expansive impulses and reach out for new population, territory, or resources nearby or farther away. Given its economic dynamism, it might turn to military aggression to achieve new gains. This possibility is by no means a necessary consequence of China's growth or of its relationship with the West, but it raises a still-unanswered question.

In *A Study of History*, Arnold Toynbee describes the nineteenth-century clash between greater industrialism and greater nationalism. He concluded that industrialism was eventually poured into nationalistic bottles in the 1890s. By 1890, the worldwide spirit of industrial change that had characterized European development from the 1820s to the 1870s no longer brought nations together or opened the channels of trade between them. Instead, that commerce became subject to higher tariffs and other restrictions. Imperialism then became the means of finding new markets and raw materials. Will military and territorial expansion be China's response to economic closure in the future?

## China's Unity

China does not have to expand to create internal unity, for it is already unified. Ninety-two percent of people in the Chinese nation are of Han Chinese descent. Minorities in Xinjiang (the Uighurs) and Tibet (the Tibetans) have had to accommodate new Hans who have been resettled there by the government. Along with the Hakka minorities in the east, these peoples have all benefited from economic growth and the rise in incomes brought about by China's dynamic industrialization.

China's unity is also very old. As the Roman Empire was fragmenting in the fourth century, China was beginning to come together as a single people. Unlike other countries, as Martin Jacques reminds us, China is a "civilization-state" in that its peoples are not polyglot—in China the cultural nation equals the state. Through time and intermarriage separate groups have become one nationality, one racial-ethnic group.[1]

If Chinese are not fully happy with one another, it is not because of ethnic differences, but because of inequality between urban and rural populations. It is generally Han rural populations that have been moved when the regime set up new coal-fired power plants or relocated people to make room for new dams, power stations, or waterways. There have been more than 100,000 acts of popular resistance against such land seizures each year.

These disputes are likely to continue because Chinese air

pollution is increasing, and not only in Beijing. Chinese water supplies are frequently contaminated by toxins owing to improper sewage and waste disposal from industrial plants. Despite an increasing ability to communicate with one another via the Internet, the Chinese population is not satisfied with the distribution of services and expresses itself clearly. Sometimes these expressions are humorous, such as the ironic song "I Love Beijing Tiananmen," an unveiled reference to student protests in 1989. Chinese Communist leaders heed these expressions of dissatisfaction, and the regime acts to placate its critics. Government polling keeps Beijing informed about people's wishes even though there are no national elections. Nevertheless, the regime has not been able to insulate itself from dissidents or divisions within the superelite. The fall of Bo Xilai in Chongqing exposed the inner workings of the Standing Committee of Nine to the outside world.

## Lineaments of Historic Change

Large-scale political institutions were in place in China by the third century B.C., long before they emerged in the West. These did not include the rule of law or political accountability. The ever-changing cavalcade of Chinese history is in large part a history of despotism. While Greeks and Romans developed a form of classical republicanism—not democracy, since many people were excluded—the classical system worked well on a small scale. As long as individuals knew and respected one another, representation in the polis or the Roman Senate could lead to effective government. When Roman territory increased and many new representatives were included, however, legislative checks were no longer effective and personal forms of despotism took their place. Unlike those of Greece and Rome, China's institutions were created to manage geographic and demographic scale. In a sense, China was the first country to create Max Weber's "bureaucracy" in which administration was extended over a huge population and territory. Bureaucrats were recruited on the basis of merit, not class or caste. But their sway was not limited by religion or rule of law as it was in the West. The doctrine of the "two swords," one spiritual and one secular, limited the power of the European state. The Christian religion emerged as a rival to state loyalties as early as the third century A.D. Ever afterward, a citizen had to balance his loyalty between the two spheres. There was no such choice in China, for no religion existed to threaten state authority. For the same reason, despotism was not limited in China. There was no "rule of law" because this was predicated on the existence of an authority superior to or at least different from the state.

In China, however, the link with ancestors—the so-called "rope of descent"—created another focus of loyalty. If a ruler was believed to represent the spirit of dead ancestors, he could command obedience. In contrast, the whole impetus of the Western tradition has been to try to substitute impartiality for nepotism in the making of political and administrative decisions. Rewarding relatives or friends was strictly forbidden, at least in theory. Martin Luther in 1517 inveighed against the Catholic practice of nepotism, rewarding relatives with offices. Subsequently, patriotism, Marxism, and Christianity each sought to persuade citizens to rise above family ties in making decisions and forming loyalties. Community norms were instilled instead.

In Britain, for example, political action and appropriate

ways of behaving have always been influenced by the monarchy and its institutional establishment—Parliament, the peerage, and the established Church of England. The general acceptance of these institutions means that the average British voter has not had to think about extreme alternatives, such as revolt, separation, or adoption of another nationality.[2] Following age-old legal precedents, citizens do what they are told when the queen's carriage rolls by. Far from being a disadvantage, the fact that so much of political life is already determined and accepted by the populace allows the typical voter to concentrate more fully on the relevant questions of the day, such as which party can best increase British economic growth or bring about a greater equality of incomes. Traditional institutions are like sausage machines—they turn out generally accepted decisions and practices that are automatic and don't need to be thought about. Because of historical acceptance of these traditional outcomes, there are few Guy Fawkeses trying to blow up the British Parliament.[3]

In China, save for the obedience to ancestors and family, state power may become unlimited. Few traditional usages govern popular practice. But Chinese power is not fully rationalized or accepted, because the "mandate of heaven" can always be withdrawn, as it was in 1911 when the Manchu dynasty fell, and again in 1949 when the Chinese Communist Party achieved power. In both cases the preexisting political system collapsed or was defeated militarily. Rejection of a Chinese regime entails exploding the overall basis of social order. In Europe, in contrast, most such changes involve new governments that still accept the antecedent pattern of authority and loyalty. Except for the period of Oliver Cromwell, the British retained the monarchy throughout their political changes. The French went from monarchy to republic but retained aspects of the old system in their transition of power.

As Francis Fukuyama demonstrates in his magisterial survey of the development of political institutions, social organizations across the globe became larger as a result of competition. Competing bands of individuals ultimately led to the formation of tribes, larger organizations. Competing tribes then produced modern states, though the process is still incomplete in Papua New Guinea and some areas of Africa.[4] Tribal kinship still retains influence in many countries. In some areas tribes have 100,000 kinsmen. Tribal bands lack the hierarchical authority of the modern state. They have to use negotiation rather than legalized force to reach agreement. As the anthropologist E. E. Evans-Pritchard has shown, in Sudan, the Nuer people continued to fight and negotiate with the Dinka (their rivals) over hundreds of years. The Chinese "rope of descent," also a remnant of tribalism, still accepts regional and familial preference and indeed corruption. Most billionaires in China are relatives of former party and state leaders: they are called "princelings."

In Europe, when religion entered the political sphere, it tended to break down old loyalties, and the multi-god classical perspective gave way to Christian monotheism. Politics then had to contend with a single competing belief system. In Roman times Christianity undermined political orthodoxy, and when it split in the sixteenth century, it further subdivided political loyalties. If all tribes agreed, one could have a very large political entity. But in Europe, they didn't. The proto-states that emerged from the Reformation did not receive their citizens' unquestioned loyalty, and they were fractured along religious lines as well as geographically. One historian contended that "the state made war, and war made the state."[5] Partly formed political entities had to fight among themselves to generate national identity and unity.

There was a large variety of political entities in sixteenth-century Europe. Empires contended with trading cities, which in turn contested with agricultural monarchies. Short of war, no form had an overwhelming advantage. It was only by means of war that the larger and more powerful agglomerations of power gradually were able to defeat smaller city-states. The same was true in China. In the late twelfth and early thirteenth centuries, Genghis Khan became the representative of effective militarism. His nomadic raiders ruled (or more properly terrorized) a huge geographic area, stretching from the Near East to Russia, Mongolia, and China. They killed, raped, and pillaged their conquests, and strains of Genghis's DNA are now found in about 8 percent of the population living in the areas he occupied. He claimed: "The greatest pleasure . . . is to vanquish your enemies and chase them before you, to rob them of their wealth and see those dear to them bathed in tears, to rob their horses and clasp to your bosom their wives and daughters."[6]

China, however, was already used to war. During the "warring states" period (also known as the Zhou period), from 770 B.C. to 256 B.C., one political unit after another battled for primacy and survival. In the end, the state of Qin—author to the Qin dynasty—prevailed and others were amalgamated within it. The battles were excruciatingly bloody. One hundred and ten political units were abolished. Sieges lasted for months and involved as many as 500,000 fighters. Warfare extended from noble chariot contests to more plebian infantry and horse attacks. Contending ideas were propounded during this struggle. Legalism—paradoxically a philosophy that undermined legal restraint—emerged to contend with Confucianism, a corpus of ideas that honored family traditions. The Qin state prevailed in part because it established a stronger link with the people by giving them land. Qin rulers also undermined the vestigial nobility. Legalism, which the Qin dynasty embraced, disparaged kin loyalties, and the regime established meritocratic recruitment for the army. This was then applied to the bureaucracy, and competitive examinations were set up for all who sought to gain office.

Fukuyama writes: "This tension between the family and the state, and the moral legitimacy that Confucianism gives to family obligations over political ones, has persisted throughout Chinese history. . . . There has been an inverse correlation between the strength of the family and the strength of the state."[7] Legalists who had little use for Confucianism believed that persons who adhered purely to family duties and values rather than abstract administrative codes should be punished. In this sense legalism was reflected in the teachings of the Chinese Communist Party after it achieved power in 1949. Legalists observed no distinction between public and private responsibilities; there was no sense of privacy; higher and lower orders were equally bound to obey the state.

The Han dynasty, established in 206 B.C., consolidated China into a unitary empire, abolishing the previous warring states. The European system of big effective states did not emerge until much later. As late as 1500 A.D. there were four hundred separate instrumentalities in European politics. Because of the greater power of large organizations, however, by 1900 these had been consolidated into twenty-five, including several overseas empires. No single dominant European state ever emerged. Europe was divided by rivers and mountain barriers; languages and dialects differed from place to place, making European unity very difficult to achieve.

The elements that prevented creation of a single polity in Europe, however, were largely absent in China. Eastern China has smoothly navigable rivers and plains. There was no powerful landed aristocracy to subdue. In Europe social and economic modernization predated formation of the modern territorial state, and trading cities offered an alternative focus. In China there was no independent commercial bourgeoisie that could claim priority over family relationships or the state. In this sense social and economic modernization didn't happen in China until much later.

There were also no formal or constitutional checks on the ruler's power. The only available sanction against a "bad emperor" was armed rebellion. This could occur only when the emperor or the dynasty had lost the "mandate of heaven." Confucius taught that the emperor had to rule in the interests of the people, but his failure to do so did not give the people a "right to revolt" in the Western or Jeffersonian sense. There was no moral authority above the regime in power. Very much later another choice appeared—the possibility of China's becoming a "trading state." China could become an exporting paradise in which growth depended on foreign trade. This possibility was created by the establishment of liberalizing coalitions under Deng Xiaoping.[8] Economic success would then take its place alongside military progress as a major objective of state policy. China after 1978 faced incentives much like those of eighteenth-century Europe. As Albert Hirschman said, in Europe "passions gave way to interests," largely defined in economic terms. The same was true in China. Mercantile interests now tell the tale in Beijing, Shanghai, and elsewhere.

But Europe reverted to imperialism and war at the end of the nineteenth century, throwing off the restraints of peaceful economic intercourse. China could do the same unless it is locked into a global Western economy in which further economic growth clearly depends on additional integration with the rest of the world.

## China's Choices

Since 1978, China's economic development has been led by expanding foreign trade. China sought markets overseas, access to capital, and raw materials, particularly oil and iron. To gain these resources, it had to open up and encourage foreign capital to enter. High economic growth followed. Still, export surpluses are not the only means of economic progress. Sooner or later China will have to promote internal development through increasing consumption by Chinese citizens. Its dependence on the outside world will lessen. At that point growth will no longer require huge foreign surpluses, because the Chinese population will buy many of the goods that otherwise would be exported, and growth rates will continue at high levels. Outsiders will have less influence on Chinese policy. As the Chinese middle class increases in size, it will also become richer and more capable of purchasing high technology and luxury goods. China will still need income from foreign trade to buy oil, natural gas, raw materials, and possibly even soybeans from abroad, but buying these materials will not require the kind of trade surplus that China has recently maintained, at around 4 percent of GDP.

Pervasive water and air pollution, however, raise questions about China's future growth. Already the world's largest producer of greenhouse gases and other pollutants, China is bringing new coal-fired plants online every month. Reducing its emissions will require new investments in carbon capture and sequestration. This means siphoning off carbon dioxide from power generation plants and piping it to underground locations where it can be stored indefinitely. Reducing emissions will add 20 percent to the cost of power generation (compared with traditional coal-fired power plants). If China manages to make its economic growth more energy efficient, it will lessen restraints on economic development. But if the energy intensity increases or remains the same, pollution controls will diminish economic growth by some 3 to 5 percent, from 10 percent to perhaps 6–7 percent growth per year. This will increase its unemployment.

International economists have also estimated contours of what has been called the "middle income trap." It has long been understood that rapid growth in a developing country cannot be sustained forever: the number of laborers peaks, causing wages to rise; it becomes harder to add new manufacturing capacity, and productivity growth tails off. Investment in new factories yields a lower return, and the economy begins to move toward services. The economist Barry Eichengreen writes: "Slowdowns coincide with the point in the growth process where it is no longer possible to boost productivity by shifting additional workers from agriculture to industry and where the gains from importing foreign technology diminish."[9] China's unusually fast growth, the aging of its population, and the very low rate of consumption as a proportion of GDP "heightens the likelihood of an imminent slowdown."

China's per capita GDP was $8,511 in 2007. At its current growth rate of 9.8 percent, it will reach $17,335 in 2015, at which point decline is likely to set in. If at this point investment remains high and consumption low, growth will fall even more.

This outcome has international implications. As wages rise and the flow of internal migrants from countryside to city declines, goods production becomes less efficient. Goods made by more expensive labor become higher priced. Even before China reached the "middle income trap," Western industries had started to bring their production home. With a further slowdown, new plants will be moved elsewhere, to Mexico, the United States, Bangladesh, Vietnam, and Thailand. The United States keeps much of the high-quality work inside its borders. Small producers especially seek hometown manufacture, where time is of the essence and quality demands are the strongest. Amazon is automating its warehouse operations with robots. The New York fashion industry is gearing up local design retailers. Here American production takes precedence over outsourcing. The price of robots designed and manufactured in the United States and Japan is rapidly declining, as Chinese labor is becoming more expensive. The two trends suggest that Chinese foreign exports and American imports will moderate with time.

In the past few years, as inflation has increased and wages have risen, Chinese entrepreneurs and state-owned industries invested an even greater proportion of GDP to stimulate exports. Investment increased from 40 percent of GDP in the 1990s to nearly 50 percent in the 2000s. Production went up, but prices also rose. Productivity peaked and then declined as it took more investment to produce the same output.[10]

This does not mean, one must stress, that Chinese growth will disappear. It will slow to about 5 percent a year, which is still higher than what the West can attain. It most assuredly does not mean that China will fail to surpass America in both gross GDP and, later, per capita GDP. Slower growth means only that the point of intersection between the two countries will be delayed.

As growth rates decline, unemployment may become a problem for the Chinese regime. Continued migration into the city can improve consumer existence and narrow the gulf between city and rural incomes. The danger is that when overall compensation stops rising rapidly, social divisions may widen. At some point Chinese citizens demand greater participation in the government decisions that affect them. When this occurred in Wilhelmine Germany in the late nineteenth century, bureaucrats and the military decided to generate enthusiasm by giving the population a great new navy. They were too successful, and it became almost impossible to restrain passage of one fleet enlargement after another. Admiral Tirpitz, the emperor, and Chancellor Bethmann Hollweg remained paralyzed as conflicts began to form with other powers whose survival was affected by unrestrained German naval building. China, in appealing to nationalism and patriotism to overcome dissent at home, may find itself in similar waters.

In China's case, the very growth of Chinese power has made civilians unhappy with any international criticism or reversal. Susan Shirk points out, "as China grew economically and militarily more powerful, nationalist emotions were spontaneously building up in the national psyche,"[11] a reaction to the country's "century of humiliation." Such sentiments are often voiced in schools and the official media. Todd Hall, a sensitive observer of China, writes: "A common oft-cited nightmare scenario is one in which the PRC regime—facing a crisis of legitimacy due to an economic downturn—stirs up aggressive, expansionist and nationalist sentiment to maintain itself in power."[12] He notes that Chinese nationalist accounts focus on three themes: "tragic separation" (the Taiwan issue); "past humiliation" (the Japan issue); and "return to glory" (renaissance in Chinese history). These stories are continually rehearsed even while China's actual benefit lies in remaining part of an essentially Western international economy.

## China and Geopolitics

As early as 1904, Halford Mackinder had attacked the notion, common in international relations, that "command of the seas" was sufficient for any Great Power to maintain its strategic leverage. Naval bombardment of ports or estuaries and "Copenhagening"—sending attack ships up an opponent's rivers to dragoon his shipping and naval vessels—were thought to give an edge to sea power over land power. In fact, as Mackinder pointed out, resources of the steppe or mountain could not be seized or interdicted by sea power. Land power, specifically railroads opening up the interior, was crucial to resource and trading dominance. Admiral Horatio Nelson's victory over the French at Trafalgar in October 1805 did not prevent Napoleon's triumph at Austerlitz two months later. Nor did sea power turn back the French invasion of Russia in 1812. Later, British dominance of the seas did not prevent the fall of France in six weeks in the spring of 1940. As Admiral Jacky Fisher always pointed out in speaking of the British: "We are fish!" and unfit to gambol on land. It followed that if great chunks of land contained the decisive population and natural resources needed for worldwide preeminence, sea power could not take or hold them.

Mackinder focused on the World Island of Eurasia—the large land mass from Calais to Kamchatka. Whoever conquered the world island, he thought, would ultimately control the world. Economic and political power outside would not be sufficient to offset it. American strategists, contemplating the possibility of a Soviet invasion of Western Europe after 1950, entertained similar notions. Eurasian power in a single pair of hands could not be matched by a combination of external states. China and Russia, of course, were the eastern projections of the world island; Europe was its western protrusion into the Atlantic. As we know, there has been a strange disequilibrium in each area's economic development: Europe has done better than Russia and China put together. This may not continue, but it is interesting to inquire why the disproportion occurred in the first place. Many theories have been given, not all of them equally convincing. Eric Jones sees the "European miracle" resulting from the subcontinent's division into parcels bordered by waterways, mountain ranges, and dense forests. These small parcels could maintain their existence because "defense" generally offset even well-prepared "offense" through most of European history. To be sure, the bringing of gunpowder from China in the twelfth and thirteenth centuries eventually led to mobile artillery and in modern times to the tracked armored vehicle with caterpillar treads—the tank—which could span trenches and small fortifications and carry firepower inland, thereby conquering large swaths of territory. Even then, some smaller states could maintain a tolerable independence by taking refuge behind mountains, seacoasts, or rivers. Securing their positions, these small political parcels engaged in a perpetual military and political competition and fostered a similar competition of ideas and economic techniques, leading to higher growth. Sustained by political independence, they could experiment with royal mercantilism or private enterprise, subsidies, or free market approaches. In Western Europe small instrumentalities like Venice, Portugal, Holland, and the members of the Hanseatic League could experiment with different strategies of advancement, testing them against one another.

In the eastern reaches of Eurasia, however, independent city-states or principalities had only a limited lifespan. Genghis Khan, sweeping across the steppe through Mongolia and into China, obliterated smaller nationalities and cast them into his empire. A millennium earlier, the Qin dynasty had triumphed over the warring states and welded them into a China that we recognize today. What Genghis and later Kublai Khan did not do, however, was to find a strategy of economic development that matched Europe's dynamism.

This was not only because of the competition imposed by a system of small states. It was also because European states freed the market from imperial control and allowed individuals to invest and profit on their own. As we have seen, European kings did not receive monolithic loyalty from their subjects but instead shared their allegiance with the Church. In England, contractual obedience to the royal master was diluted by King John's contract with the nobles in the Magna Carta of 1215. Religious and legal symbols competed with royal authority and legitimacy. And of course, if one did not like the rule in France, one could move to Holland or England. One did not have to travel far to find another and possibly more tolerable realm of authority. Economic experimentation thus facilitated economic growth. China was poised to undergo the Industrial Revolution in 1750 but did not do so, because its agricultural production was still backward and required a huge number of peasants to work in the fields. Britain, in contrast, had an agricultural revolution and could reduce its farming population and send many tillers to the cities to join the industrial workforce. China remained a subsistence economy for two more centuries.

Now China has emulated the rest of the world and gained great power and authority on the Eastern reaches of the Eurasian continent, the World Island. It is doing less well than it did ten years ago. Its exports are declining and imports increasing. Its newly acquired middle-class status, as well as air and water pollution, will restrain growth. Reduction in the use of fossil fuels will also reduce the rate of growth. Citizens used to high growth and rising incomes will be less satisfied. The Communist Party may then have to mitigate its growing unpopularity either by opening up and democratizing—a risky strategy—or by humming the nationalist patriotic tune at the expense of other powers. But despite the risks, democratization would allow China to ensure its own industrial future by increasing ties with the enhancing market that the resurgent West will offer.

China's economic growth will slow for a variety of reasons, but these will not place it on a similar footing with the United States. China will still pass the United States, but its industrial future will be tied to links with Western capitalism that, if severed, will dictate Chinese decline.

# EIGHT

# *Alternatives*

Previous interpretive or policy approaches to the problems of East-West rivalry do not obviate the analysis provided here. Some commentators claim that the United States can cope with the economic and political-military challenges it faces without any help. Or they assert that China and the West are doomed to eventual war, or that nothing can be done but bow to China's inevitable ascendancy and we must resign ourselves to whatever international steps the People's Republic chooses to take. Of course, those who believe all is well and nothing need be done offer some qualifications to their conclusion. The United States requires allies, and other countries will support it. China itself does not pose a major threat because it has been "globalized" and therefore acts more or less responsibly within the global system.

Those who take this view cannot explain why in response to China's growth other nations and federations are seeking additional size and garnering new allies. The answer is that the world is not fully open, and Western nations cannot export their goods to developing Asia. In Beijing's case, Western industry must produce there with Chinese partners. If it had been otherwise the Doha Round of international tariff cutting would have succeeded and led to a more open world economy. It did not, and as things stand now, it will not. East Asians do not want foreign goods surging into their markets to provide for growing domestic needs. Asian nations want to serve their populations and domestic consumption by themselves. This means that Western exports have to find a larger arena without relying on Asia. Because the world does not have an open economy, nations have negotiated one customs union after another to create the economic size that they otherwise lack. Some 40 free-trade agreements, mostly bilateral, have been reached since 1980. The United States itself is in 20 of these and Europe 26. According to the World Trade Organization, 319 free-trade agreements are currently in force, and 200 more have been proposed.

Joining with others does not mean that individual countries cannot do anything to mitigate their decline. They can replace deteriorating infrastructure and educational systems. They can admit new immigrants: as population rises, domestic demand will increase. They can enhance their investments in technology. All these measures would augment growth and incomes. It is unlikely however, that they would fully counterbalance China's growth. Relative decline would still be with us. Even if China's growth sinks to 5 percent, it will still exceed America's 3 percent.

In short, America needs a strong partner. Some will claim that China itself, East Asia, or India can be that partner. In the longer term they may be right. But for now, neither China nor India is interested in joining economically with a declining, or even decadent United States. Each is doing well on its own and does not see a need for assistance or economic allies. Their growth is high; their exports bound ahead; their productivity and costs should remain competitive for the next ten years. They do not want to open their markets to Western industrial goods, and they have little need for investment or markets beyond those now available.

Another option is for America to bow to its apparently inevitable descent and take a back seat in world politics. Though China is not yet democratic, it possesses economically liberal instincts and seems to want to advance through trade, not conquest. The United States can associate with this new proponent of globalization and share in the benefits. It can then take a less military approach to foreign relations and withdraw from some of its exposed positions in Iraq, Afghanistan, and elsewhere. The peace dividend from reducing military expenditure will help cut the deficit and make more funds available for education, research, and high technology. And peacetime investment would help create employment.

This is all true and would hold regardless of America's strategic position. But the United States can strengthen its position by joining with others. Economic confederation provides a stimulus that America otherwise lacks. New demand, a greater market, and access to international funds and technology are only some of the benefits that would accrue from a new economic relationship with the European Union and eventually with Japan. The economic magnet of a market three times larger than that of the United States cannot be achieved in isolation. Nor can it come about by cutting tariffs with East

Asia, Africa, Latin America, or the Middle East. None of these regions are ready to reduce tariffs on American or European goods. The failure of trade liberalization under the World Trade Organization makes this very clear.

## A Direct Rapprochement with China

In the past several years the United States has tried to improve its position by seeking to create a G2 with China, which has been uninterested and unimpressed. There are too many present disagreements with Beijing—on trade, currency manipulation, global warming, military measures, and territorial claims—for the two governments to reach a more general accommodation. The United States does not presently have the negotiating cards to make an approach to China credible or successful. It is weak in its trade balance, spending, and governmental response to crisis. China has recovered from the 2008–9 recession, but the United States still suffers from high unemployment and tepid growth. Moreover, the United States has close relations with some traditional Chinese enemies: Japan, India, a rejuvenated Taiwan, South Korea, and Indonesia. China senses the historical rivalry of rising and declining powers in world politics and is unwilling to submerge its claims to reach agreement with America. Nor is it clear that the Chinese population would want it to. At the very least, agreement will be put off between Beijing and Washington.[1]

Regardless, some might say, an agreement with Europe is not now in the cards. The European Union has its hands full. The Greek crisis might spread to Italy, Portugal, and Spain. The monetary union must be buttressed by a fiscal union before the euro can be fully safeguarded. Until then, no new countries (except perhaps Iceland) should be admitted to the union.

Such a response, however, would be shortsighted. On Europe's eastern frontiers, the Russian Federation is beckoning eastern states to join its customs and currency agreement. Belarus, Ukraine, Moldova, Kazakhstan, and Georgia are thus up for grabs. Azerbaijan and Armenia are isolated, but Russia is trying to entice them into a federal relationship with Moscow. If the European Union simply rests on its oars, deeply divided countries like Ukraine may be drawn back into the Russian orbit. It therefore appears likely that the European Union will extend its Neighborhood Policy (ENP) and its political mantle to include countries on the Kremlin's list. After a measure of democratic reforms, these countries will become candidates to join the European Union. The financial and debt crisis besetting Eastern Europe will not form a permanent barrier to the admission of these states.

Other critics propose that the United States do nothing because it is in fine shape. While China moves ahead in terms of gross domestic product, its per capita GDP still lags. Its suppressed inflation and the covert indebtedness of its banks make it vulnerable to a new economic crisis. Underperforming loans will eventually have to be acknowledged and downgraded. China's state-owned enterprises received capital at the direction of political leaders but may not be able to repay their loans. Total Chinese indebtedness, therefore, is as large or larger than American. China's research and development is also deficient and is not being improved. It has to buy technology to keep up, and as the accidents with high-speed rail demonstrate, Chinese authorities do a poor job of implementing European and Japanese technology on their own soil. Undertrained workers may not form roadbeds or lay tracks well enough to sustain the very high speeds these trains are designed to reach.

In the longer term, the aging of the Chinese population will reduce the number of workers per retiree, possibly compromising the future security of Chinese elders. Pollution of air and water will make some urban areas almost unlivable as farmers move in from the countryside. Coal-fired generation plants may come to control sulfur dioxide, but they do not yet divert carbon dioxide to underground storage sites. Effluent from chemical industries still pours into Chinese waterways. China will have to cut its growth rate to get control of its pollution.

Nor does the Chinese educational system match its Western competitors. Though ostensibly training a large number of engineers, most of these people are more accurately described as technicians. They cannot yet compete with their industrial colleagues elsewhere, particularly in formulating new products. They duplicate rather than innovate. But reverse engineering will not sustain China's challenge any more than it did its Soviet counterpart in years past.[2]

These claims all have some validity, but overall they should not persuade Americans to neglect China's rise and the challenge that goes with it. China's research and development is deficient, but this has not prevented a considerable increase in industrial productivity in the past decade. Its wages have risen, and China is rapidly becoming a middle-class nation.[3] Its growth rates have slowed down and will recede further, but this does not suggest a Japanese-style "lost decade" in which growth declines to 0–1 percent per year. Over 30 percent of Chinese people work in agriculture. As this figure falls below 10 percent, as it has done in every developed country, China will benefit from an infusion of new labor to engage in industrial projects, and its cities and manufacturing capabilities will enlarge. Nor does China's political system impede its development. The central regime and its provincial chiefs have worked together to keep up with the West and Japan. The flow of Chinese students into and out of Western cities and institutions of learning has communicated a wide range of information on Western activities and plans. In the United States and elsewhere, Chinese scholars have contributed to the highest levels of achievement and have been recognized for their work. Returning to China, they have been able to keep up their research and technological progress in mainland institutions. China currently holds twelve Nobel Prizes, and its work in science and technology is outstanding.

While not emulating previous challengers, China has somewhat inadvertently followed Germany's route of the nineteenth century—developing within the context of an overarching world economy, but focusing as well on military expenditure and armaments. Its expanded territorial concerns are not unlike those of Berlin under Kaiser Wilhelm II. In 1914 Britain did not respond effectively to deflect the German challenge and Germany did not assuage Britain's concerns. The "balance of power" did not prevent war but brought it on. One certainly does not want to repeat this outcome in the relation between China and the United States.

## A Congressional Blockage

Some readers may wonder whether the U.S. Congress as presently constituted would ever extend a hand of economic linkage and friendship to the European Union. It should be remembered, however, that most E.U. members (except Sweden, Finland, and Ireland) are also members of the North Atlantic Treaty Organization.[4] The relationship with the United States is firmly established and NATO (like the E.U.) has broadened its membership by including new states from Eastern Europe. Congress has proved that it can extend free-trade agreements to other countries as long as labor protections are included. These might also be worked out with the European Union, as E.U. countries already share American labor standards. Unlike when it made its pact with South Korea, the United States would not have to worry that low-wage European countries would undercut the American labor market, because labor in Europe is more expensive than in the United States. It is more likely that E.U. countries would object to a free-trade arrangement with the United States on grounds that American debt could suck further European capital into the United States. Given today's high levels of capital mobility, however, that prospect has already been faced and accounted for. Furthermore, Angela Merkel, speaking for her European colleagues, has already proposed such a union between Europe and the United States.

It is true that both Europe and the United States are inward looking. Domestic problems are more salient than those outside: jobs, technology, education, and investment lag on both continents. Europeans and Americans are both hesitant to embrace new external tasks, surfeited as they are with unsolved internal problems. But in both cases (as in the Cold War), it is the international challenge that will call forth new efforts at unity. NATO and the European Union prospered in the face of the Soviet challenge. Internal strength grew on both sides of the Atlantic. Some claimed that the end of the Cold War would turn both NATO and the E.U. into pointless alliances without a clear direction. But economic and political factors now call for a unification of the West to achieve larger goals in both realms. Neither Europe nor the United States can sustain itself without the greater economic and political size their union would provide. It would bring in demand and a larger supply of funds and manufacturing capability to meet it. Between 1945 and 1973 both Europe and North America found a huge stimulus in deferred consumption and revived investment. Globalization and trade rebounded. As the United States opened its doors to European and Japanese exports, industrial nations sought and achieved new and higher standards of living. In the 1990s new nations entering the West after the collapse of the Soviet Empire deepened and spread prosperity.

Growth later declined, of course, and prosperity was interrupted by an economic bubble in 2000 and a deep recession in 2008. But these were a reflection of finance's spurious and unsustainable victory over the manufacturing industries. Such victories will not take place again, as capital and educated labor move back to manufacturing and other service industries. The current inequality of incomes placed money in the hands of the very rich, the least likely to spend it. Historical trends suggest a move to more equal compensation over time.

In the future, incomes are likely to flatten, and previously less developed economies will grow, some of them joining the OECD. That greater inclusion has already embraced Asia; it will soon spread beyond Eastern Europe to the Caucasus, North Africa, and perhaps the Middle East. Hundreds of millions of individuals in Africa have been excluded from a modern existence because of bad internal governance and inadequate education. North Africa, parts of the Arabian Peninsula, and even Central Asian states may ultimately start to plumb Western markets for sophisticated consumer goods. These changes will boost world demand for the West's output. The East will also benefit, but a retooled Western industry will be the vital spark to lagging consumption internationally, particularly on the fringes of Europe. It will also provide the technological underpinning for Chinese exports. A unification of the West may not occur as soon as it should. In the aftermath of the great recession, most countries' politics are focused on public and private debt and deficient growth. Unemployment needs to be remedied in country after country, especially in Europe, where it is higher than in the United States. Many nations have overspent their budgets or undertaxed their citizens for a long time. Deficit countries have to hold back and surplus countries have to increase their purchasing and domestic consumption. A worldwide rebalancing requires much greater Chinese expenditure; rebalancing within the West demands German economic expansion, which means buying products from less-wealthy countries in its midst.

As John Maynard Keynes understood, countries cannot transfer funds to another state unless they have an export surplus that permits them to do so.[5] If Germany does not permit Eastern European exports to enter, it must spend its long-term capital on investments in Eastern Europe as a substitute. Berlin complains about extravagant government spending in Italy and Greece, but it should recognize that this has spectacularly lowered the value of the euro, causing a boon for German exporters selling overseas. If Greek profligacy did not exist, it would have to be invented. Now Berlin must rebalance the equation within Europe and the eurozone.

## Should America Break Up?

Some believe that the euro should fail and the eurozone break up, restoring individual nations' monetary sovereignty. People making this argument must consider the rationale for a single currency in the first place and monetary practice in the United States. Would not California or Massachusetts like to depreciate its own state currency to get back into balance with other states and send exports to the rest of the union? In theory they might, but this would vitiate the very reason for having a common currency in the United States of America in the first place. Under the Articles of Confederation before a single currency existed, industrial producers in Massachusetts could not be sure they would get value for money in sending their textiles to Virginia in return for debased Dutch currency or later the continental. With no federal authority over the currency and competing centers of issuance, one could get a currency "not worth a continental." For economic development to proceed, both Massachusetts and California needed to use the same standard of value in their exchanges with each other. Essentially the argument for the euro in Europe is the same as the argument for the dollar in the United States—it facilitates the movements of factors of production, trade, and labor among countries and thus increases economic growth. In Europe a country wishing to partake in this movement of factors will also want to be part of the eurozone, unless, like Switzerland or England, its currency remains highly valued in external terms. Switzerland and the United Kingdom are known for the external trade and the quality of their visible and invisible exports. But a Slovenia may not have these advantages and may need to demonstrate its willingness to accept and repay its investment in hard currency. How many pension funds around the world would replace their euro investments with those in drachmas or Finn marks? How many Americans would prefer a California currency to federal greenbacks?

Of course there are alternatives to the vision sketched here.

The default option of doing nothing has been history's typical recourse. Rarely have nations and peoples possessed the possibility of altering their fortunes in basic terms. The international system sets implacable limits on change. Only after a war or economic crisis do nations' horizons rise to consider a fundamental alteration in the way of doing international business. Now is such a time. Competitors exist who may turn into enemies, but the world can transcend this danger through larger-scale agglomerations of power in world politics, bringing in their potential foe or foes. The possibility of an enduring overbalance of power lies before us. It needs only to be seized upon.

## Conclusion

Despite the existence of hesitant or adverse views, the vision offered here is both feasible and necessary for Western renewal. It is consistent with the strictures of European and American politics, and it emphasizes the need to bring larger demand and higher technology to the two great Western economies. No purely national stimulus will be sufficient. In the nineteenth century American expansion brought a new demand for goods from populations in the western United States. Despite the current recession and low growth, new economies joining Europe contribute to the demand for industrial products from European factories and mines. The achievement of larger scale stimulates economic growth on both sides of the Atlantic.

# NINE

# How the West Attracts China and the World

## The Meaning of the West

There is no satisfactory definition of "the West." It is not a purely geographic phenomenon because easterly located nations like Australia, New Zealand, and South Africa have Western institutions and religious backgrounds. If the Greenwich meridian were taken as a border between East and West, almost all of Europe would be consigned to the East: West would then be limited to the Western Hemisphere. If the possession of high-technology industry is the appropriate standard for membership in the West, the OECD (the official determiner of Western status) would, as it does, include Japan and South Korea in its number. If British parliamentary institutions are the signal characteristic, then India has to be included as institutionally Western, but not the United States. But India is also unique. In India, English is the lingua franca because Bengalis do not speak Hindi, and Hindus are ignorant of the tongue of their eastern countrymen.

Samuel Huntington located a civilizational divide between Western and Eastern Christianity on the borders of Serbia, Poland, and Russia: Catholic Croatians were Western, and Russian Orthodox Serbs Eastern. Yet differences within Christianity do not compare with those between Hindus and Westerners, Chinese Buddhists and English Christians. As Francis Fukuyama makes clear, absolutism versus limited government and the rule of law mark another important historical distinction between Eastern and Western states.

East clearly can become West over time. Japan remains culturally distinct, but its economic and political institutions make it the West's Eastern terminus. Just as the Eastern Europe of Soviet days could become Western as it joined the European Union, so too could Turkey, a Muslim state, progressively incline itself toward Europe with democratic institutions to match.[1] This is precisely the transformation Karl Deutsch observed as he saw rural Bretons and Gascons begin to speak the same language and become Frenchmen. Eugen Weber also underscored the emotional shift that occurred when peasants merged with urban members of the French middle class to become one French nation.[2] In Deutsch's view, this transition took place rapidly between 1789 and 1799 as the flow of national messages overwhelmed purely provincial communications. Modernization is first a nationalizing and then an internationalizing phenomenon as it broadens the pattern of essential communications within and then between states. Rudyard Kipling notwithstanding, East may meet West.

For present purposes, traditional definitions will have to

suffice: the East starts at the Russian border and extends to the Bering Strait. The West includes all of Europe, North and South America, and Alaska. These borders are certainly mutable, as erstwhile Communist states join the European Union and "West" moves east to include Japan.

## International Processes

As we know, "West" and "East" represent distinctive cultures and economic systems that may not join together. This does not mean that they cannot approximate one another or move closer together. Over the past two decades, the forces of globalization and the spread of democratic values have inclined many states to orient more toward the West. The international trading system's rules have been accepted by such nominally non-Western nations as Japan, Korea, and increasingly China. If Karl Deutsch is right, changes in patterns of communication will bring them closer still.

Yet as one observes patterns of international government, there has so far been no ultimate linking of East and West. The United Nations, the Security Council, the General Assembly, the G-7 and the G-20 have not brought a lasting accommodation among their members. Each of these forums allows discussion, but few produce agreement. When agreements are achieved, as the record of the U.N. Security Council shows, they are at the most minimal, common-denominator level. Few U.N.-approved sanctions bite against designated aggressors or deviant states. The G-7 (without either Russia or China as members) has occasionally improved economic decisions among purely Western powers. But these are not shared with leading Eastern nations (except Japan).

## The Theory of Institutionalism

There are broadly three different theoretical approaches to international order or governance. The first, propounded by realists as well as the English analyst Hedley Bull, holds that order emerges out of the relations of power. Norms may emerge from this approach, but they depend on balance-of-power resistance to militant aggression in world politics. From this standpoint, even war is an attempt to achieve "order" among nation-states. The First and Second World Wars are measures of systemic sanctions meted out to those who would upset the legitimate existing order. The return to an overall "balance" did not occur after 1918 but did after 1945. Since then, nations have operated within a generally peaceful system, beset or occasionally interrupted by quarrels among lesser powers.

Given the development of an overbalance of power, it was possible to conclude the Cold War without recourse to force. The problem of using the balance of power as the major guarantor and protector of international order, however, is that it relies on the disorder of military force to gain the ultimate objective. Countless people are killed in the name of reestablishing order among nations and countries. It is an unsatisfactory response to the existence of anarchy in the international system.

The second response has been more peaceful, but generally ineffective. At the end of major conflicts like the First and Second World Wars nations set up large international organizations to prevent further war. The creation of the United Nations in October 1945 brought some fifty nations together, but the Security Council and the General Assembly operated on different principles. In the General Assembly, decisions could be taken by majority vote. In the Security Council results effectively depended on the agreement of the Big Five (Russia, China, the United States, Britain, and France), each of which could issue a veto. The General Assembly thus became a talk shop in which decisions could not be enforced without the Security Council's agreement. Ideological conflicts prevented the Great Powers from agreeing on most questions. Thus, all-encompassing international institutions, dealing with issues across the board, faced major difficulties in directing or even influencing international events.

Emerging from the frustrations of the worldwide institutional attempts at governance, organizations with more focused responsibilities came to the fore. The World Bank, the World Trade Organization, and the International Monetary Fund each concentrated attention on trade and monetary matters. The World Bank sought to help the developing countries. The World Trade Organization sought to reduce tariffs and controls on commerce. The International Monetary Fund dealt with exchange rates and the means of easing balance-of-payments problems. In theory it was supposed to provide finance to get an indebted country out of its difficulties without having to depreciate its currency or put on tariffs or controls. Aid from the IMF could be conditioned on reforms by the indebted nation such as higher interest rates, or reduced government spending. In return, the IMF might accept a devaluation of the affected nation's currency. Further aid would depend on the receiving nation living up to its commitments. In general terms the IMF's objective was to prevent a closure of the international economic system; it stood ready to advance capital to prevent major countries from defaulting on their debts, as happened, for example, with the collapse of Austria in 1931. That default caused contagion in Germany and later England and the world at large, transforming a local crisis into the derangement of the entire international financial system. In contrast to other international organizations, the IMF has carried out its writ quite effectively, though it has not uniformly prevented financial default. Russia defaulted in 1998 and Argentina in 2001. The IMF, buttressing the European Central Bank, has helped to avoid a default in Greece and Italy. No major European or Asian country has suffered collapse from a lack of IMF assistance. The United States and the IMF act together because America has a veto on the extension of IMF credit. But the IMF does not handle political or military matters and has only a limited diplomatic role.

The G-7 or G-8 (with Russia attending) has focused attention on international economic relations between the major economies. The United States, Germany, Japan, Canada, France, Britain, and Italy have focused on major economic issues, but nonmarket economies (like China's) have not been allowed to join. Therefore, the conclusions reached by either body do not have legitimacy across the international system as a whole.

The G-20, a new and overlarge aggregation, was set up to bring in nonmarket-oriented economies. It had the advantage of including India and China as well as Brazil, Argentina, Australia, South Africa, Indonesia, Saudi Arabia, and Mexico. But it was too unwieldy to reach agreement on concrete issues. Because of the diversity of membership, the proposals it has made, for instance, to continue the Kyoto Protocol on energy, have been excessively vague and imprecise. No countries committed themselves to specific reductions in the production of greenhouse gases, and China and India still insisted on greater leeway as developing countries. The result again had the deficiency of aiming for a least-common-denominator standard of achievement.

## Sequential Adherence

At the end of a major conflict, nations are used to sitting down and creating a new organization that will prevent the previous crisis. All of the victors participate and largely dictate terms to the losers. The result is a skewed organization that, though large in scale, is not universally accepted as legitimate by the losers and bystanders. The peace of Utrecht after the War of Spanish Succession in 1713 ended the challenge of Louis XIV but did not assimilate France to the existing international system. France could rise again to challenge English and Dutch pretensions, as it did under Napoleon. The Vienna settlement of 1815 was in comparison a "Goldilocks" agreement.[3] Not too much and not too little, it restrained France but brought it back into the international system. It essentially got French agreement to a lasting Great Power settlement, which endured until the revolutions of 1848 upset the applecart of the "legitimate" order. In 1919, the Versailles Treaty, worked out in Paris over the course of the first months of that year, violated traditional notions of fittingness and restraint. By blaming Germany for the war, taking away a slew of German territories, and demanding excessive reparations, the treaty assaulted the German people and laid the groundwork for its own demise in later years. The peace after 1945 did neither of these. As the victors over Germany split apart, the end of World War II provided no lasting accommodation of the Great Powers; it set up an emasculated United Nations that operated fitfully when the Big Five could come together.

Responding to the rise of the Cold War, however, European nations began creating an independent economic and political force fundamentally linked to the United States of America. It was an inchoate attempt at reassembly of the West in both political and military terms. It also represented the consolidation of an overbalance of power to counter the possibility of a Soviet move to dominate the globe.

What was more interesting, perhaps, was how the reassembly was accomplished. The six original nations laid down a common market with the intention of ultimately transforming it into a more integrated organization that would draw in other members of the European family. The key to the Common Market and later the European Union, however, was not the number of states involved but the intent to create a core of countries that were willing to merge their sovereignties into something greater. The core would regulate and determine who else could join. They were interested only in those who would accept the acquis communautaire of commitment to the integrated whole. The strength of this approach was that it did not represent a "least common denominator" demarche. Instead of getting twenty-seven countries together and asking for the minimum they might permit, the "core approach" mandated that each new joiner had to agree to a high level of obligation, or it could not join. The late joiners did not set the terms; they were set by a preexisting core of powerful states. Therefore it was possible to combine a large number of new members with increasing integration over time. Indeed, higher integration was required because twenty-seven states could no longer rely on unanimity to make decisions. Thus the broadening of integration also entailed its deepening. Common internal free trade led to a common external tariff. An exchange rate regime led to a common currency. The establishment of a European Central Bank led essentially to a fiscal union with powers to curtail or even direct national budget spending. If countries were members of the eurozone, they had to deal with the problems of countries that had trouble meeting their payments. Each step of integration made further steps necessary.

## International Agglomeration

Can the methods applied within the West be extended outside its ambit? In theory international agglomeration has always been available as the alternative to a balance of power. A peace could be achieved "in parts";[4] that is, an integrated arrangement already in place could be extended to others. In practice, however, conflict was restrained by a buildup of alliances or armaments to maintain equilibrium. But when agglomeration works, it prevents war and the associated expense of large arms races. After 1815, the European great powers had the choice of continuing to oppose a nationalist France or drawing France into a continental combination in which all members would commit to maintaining territorial and political stability. Instead of using "balancing techniques," Metternich, Castlereagh, and Tsar Alexander I coopted France, which was led by Talleyrand and Louis XVIII. They saved enormous sums by creating an overpowering coalition that constrained France from within. Bismarck did much the same thing between 1871 and 1890: he created a coalition of three or four major powers so large that France, though territorially dissatisfied, did not try to fashion an aggressive balance against him. After 1890, however, as we have seen, an even balance of Triple Alliance and Triple Entente failed to restrain either side, a failure that led directly to World War I.

In 1945, Franklin D. Roosevelt tried to bring Josef Stalin into an accord involving four policemen (China, the United States, the Soviet Union, and Britain), but it could not be maintained, and a balance pitting Eastern Communist regimes against Western democracies followed. Later, Dwight D. Eisenhower and John F. Kennedy built up a coalition that was de facto superior to any possible Soviet phalanx. That overbalance of power eventually registered, and Mikhail Gorbachev sought agreement to bring Russia into the larger group. This attempt only partially succeeded. Russia's reforms remained incomplete.

The worlds of today and tomorrow offer two possibilities for dealing with China as an emerging power. One is the traditional balance, with all the military and economic wastage that such a course would involve. The second is drawing China into a broader coalition that is too large for China to balance against. Overweening power can act as a magnet. Could the methods of the European Union, successful in the West, be used to attract China to a larger combination of nations? Such an approach would have the disadvantage that it could not in practice be worldwide. That two hundred nations would or could join seems impossible or doubtful, at least in the first instance. But that does not mean that like-minded states could not agree to peace and economic solidarity with one another: it depends on the incentives. Tariff blocs can attract one another in a way that nonintegrated states cannot do. They already have internal free trade, a common currency, and common fiscal approaches. The question is whether a second great power or group of states needs to benefit from participating in the first's bloc. If it does, integration can take place on a multilateral and even multicultural basis as the progressive addition of Japan to the West manages to do. If the United States and Europe formed a customs union—a transatlantic free-trade alliance, or TAFTA—that would affect the trade of nations in the Far East, used to selling their final goods in the Western market. A free-trade bloc in the West would mean barriers to the East that could be transcended only by one or more Eastern countries pledging to join. A purely Western union would bring about $37 trillion of goods and services together and 800 million people. If Japan joined, this would add nearly $10 trillion in value and more than 100 million in population to their number, concentrating more than half of world GDP in a single coalition.

What then would be the policy of a nationalist and authoritarian China? It would of course not meet the political and legal requirements to join. But China's long-term economic future might depend on continuing association with Western markets and technology. The process would be akin to that applied to prospective members of the European Union. An authoritarian Serbia could not join, but a democratic Slovenia could. A Greece run by colonels could not join, but democratic Greece was admitted later. An open economy and the pervasive rule of law governing transactions and political liberties would have to be achieved. These standards are not impossible ones: they have influenced change in Spain, Portugal, Greece, Turkey, Bulgaria, Romania, Hungary, and elsewhere. Even strife-ridden Bosnia may yet become a member. Who is therefore to say that China could never join a TAFTA that already included the United States of America, the European Union, and, in a trans-Pacific accretion, Japan? Deng Xiaoping in-spired China to undergo an economic revolution in 1978. A later Chinese leader can fashion an economic and political revolution to join with the West in the twenty-first century. If that takes place, the power of economic and political at-traction will create a foundation so strong that warfare among great powers will become a thing of the past. The accretion of greater economic and political size in international politics will fashion a core of peaceful states that withstands the ubiquitous temptation to collide with one another. Internationalism will have overcome nationalism through a gradual agglomeration of integrated power. This potent amalgam with China, the last but essential ingredient, represents an attainable and lasting vision of international peace.

# Notes

1. As of 2011, U.S. companies were holding $1.8 trillion in idle balances. See *Financial Times*, "Wealth," June 24, 2011, p. 52.

2. For the economic advantages, see particularly Klaus Desmet and Stephen L. Parente, "Bigger Is Better: Market Size, Demand Elasticity, and Innovation," *International Economic Review* 51, no. 2 (May 2010): 319–33.

3. This may raise political difficulties in internal politics. Hays, Ehrlich, and Peinhardt write: "Because trade causes economic dislocations and exposes workers to greater risk, it generates political opposition that democratically elected leaders ignore at their peril. Thus . . . political leaders have had to be aware of and actively manage public support for economic openness. To do this, governments have exchanged welfare state policies that cushion their citizens from the vagaries of the international economy in return for public support for openness." Quoted in Ronald Findlay and Kevin O'Rourke, *Power and Plenty* (Princeton, N.J.: Princeton University Press, 2007), p. 538.

4. See particularly W. Brian Arthur, *The Nature of Technology* (New York: Free Press, 2009), especially chapter 10.

CHAPTER I. THE SIZE OF STATES

1. One observer comments: "the larger the economy, the higher the level of welfare . . . which results from the larger diversity of products and the higher rate of innovation."

2. Findlay and O'Rourke, *Power and Plenty;* Crane Brinton, *From Many One: The Process of Political Integration, the Problem of World Government* (Cambridge: Harvard University Press, 1948).

3. See F. Crouzet, "Aggression and Opulence," in *Leading the World Economically,* ed. Francois Crouzet and Armand Clesse (Amsterdam: Dutch University Press, 2003).

4. Brinton, *From Many One.*

5. See Ronald Findlay, "Towards a Model of Territorial Expansion and the Limits of Empire," in *The Political Economy of Conflict and Appropriation,* ed. Michelle R. Garfinkle and Stergios Skaperdas (New York: Cambridge University Press, 1996).

6. See Geoffrey Parker, *The Army of Flanders and the Spanish Road, 1567–1659: The Logistics of Spanish Victory and Defeat in the Low Countries' Wars* (Cambridge: Cambridge University Press, 2004).

7. "A closer study of NATO confirms . . . the expectation that democratic states can form a security community that is based on the same democratic principles as that are governing their domestic political systems." Helene Sjursen, *On the Identity of NATO* (London: Royal Institute of International Affairs, Blackwell, 2004), p. 689.

8. "The spice trade, based on the intense need for pepper and other spices to preserve meat in Europe, had been a lucrative one for centuries. . . . It was the basis for . . . unparalleled wealth . . . of the Great Maritime Republic [Venice] jealously guarded against the encroachments of its rival, Genoa." Ronald Findlay, "The Roots of Divergence: Western Economic History in Comparative Perspective," *American Economic Review* 82, no. 2 (May 1992).

9. Richard Freeman, "Are Your Wages Set in Beijing?" *Journal of Economic Perspectives* (Summer 1995): 17–19.

10. See Alberto Alesina and Enrico Spolaore, *The Size of Nations* (Cambridge: MIT Press, 2003).

11. Karl August Wittvogel, *Oriental Despotism: A Comparative Study of Total Power* (New Haven, Conn.: Yale University Press, 1957).

12. Mary Boatwright, Daniel Gargola, and Richard Talbert, *The Romans: From Village to Empire* (Oxford: Oxford University Press, 2004), p. 136.

13. Pope Gregory I asserted, "Let the terrestrial kingdom serve—or be the slave—of the celestial" (Unam Sanctum). "The primacy of the church over the state allowed it to acquire temporal power in the West in the eighth

century, when the popes cut their ties with Byzantium." Deepak Lal, *Unintended Consequences: The Impact of Factor Endowments, Culture, and Politics on Long-Run Economic Performance* (Cambridge: MIT Press, 1998), p. 78.

14. See Mancur Olson, *Power and Prosperity: Outgrowing Communist and Capitalist Dictatorships* (Oxford: Oxford University Press, 2000).

15. "Venice was the first city in the Middle Ages to live by trade alone." Robert-Henri Bautier, *The Economic Development of Medieval Europe* (New York: Harcourt Brace Jovanovich, 1971), p. 65.

16. Robert S. Lopez, "The Trade of Medieval Europe: The South," *Cambridge Economic History of Europe*, vol. 2 (Cambridge: Cambridge University Press, 1987).

17. Samuel E. Morison and Henry Steele Commager, *The Growth of the American Republic*, vol. 1 (New York: Oxford University Press, 1950), on the problem of imperial organization.

18. Bouda Etemad, *Possessing the World: Taking the Measurements of Colonisation from the Eighteenth to the Twentieth Century* (New York: Berghahn Books, 2007).

19. Sally Marks, *The Ebbing of European Ascendancy: An International History of the World, 1914–1945* (London: Arnold; New York: Oxford University Press, 2002).

20. Many states with large economies like Japan, China, European nations, and even the United States substituted non-tariff barriers to compensate for their reductions in the Tokyo Round of tariff cuts.

21. *New York Times*, April 30, 2011, p. B1.

22. Some small states like Taiwan, Israel, Singapore, and others survived by developing defense relationships with bigger powers.

CHAPTER 2. THE RISE OF THE EAST

1. W. Arthur Lewis writes: "The period 1880–1913 has to be regarded as one in which many tropical countries grew as rapidly as many of the industrial countries." Quoted in Findlay and O'Rourke, *Power and Plenty*, p. 415.

2. Hans Singer among others argued that the terms of trade had turned against developing countries.

3. Findlay and O'Rourke write: "Import substitution may have permitted initial growth spurts in many developing countries, but eventually domestic markets became saturated and growth declined" (p. 526). See also Bela Balassa et al., *Development Strategies in Semi-Industrial Economies* (London: World Bank, 1982).

4. The power and handling of the Datsun 280Z, however, proved that Nissan could hack it anywhere.

5. See Raymond Vernon, *Sovereignty at Bay* (New York: Basic, 1971).

6. The *Economist* writes: "As the number of people directly employed in making things declines, the cost of labour as a proportion of the total cost of production will diminish too. This will encourage makers to move some of the work back to rich countries." "The Third Industrial Revolution," April 21, 2012, p. 4.

7. See Ezra Vogel, *Deng Xiaoping and the Transformation of China* (Cambridge: Harvard University Press, 2011).

8. See Richard Baum, *Burying Mao: Chinese Politics in the Age of Deng Xiaoping* (Princeton, N.J.: Princeton University Press, 1996).

9. Paul Krugman, "The Myth of Asia's Miracle," *Foreign Affairs* 73, no. 6 (November–December 1994): 62–78.

10. Mengkui Wang, ed., *China in the Wake of Asia's Financial Crisis* (Abingdon, Oxon, and New York : Routledge, 2009), p. 64.

11. China still faces major trade-offs between free movement of capital, exchange rates, and interest rates. As economists have shown, government can exercise only two of three options. Until now, China has tried to manipulate both its exchange rate and interest rates, and this has meant that capital flows were not free to enter and leave the country. The Bank of China "sterilizes" incoming funds so that they do not end up in people's pockets to buy imports or to increase consumption. If China allowed its exchange rate to fluctuate freely, its monetary policy would be determined by capital flows that would enter or leave the country when the renminbi rose or fell. A fall in the domestic monetary base would push interest rates up. In practice China has kept its exchange rate relatively fixed, allowing the Bank of China freely to move interest rates up and down. This policy, however, is not likely to last.

12. Professor Benjamin Friedman has argued that the high rate of Chinese economic development would normally have involved progressive democratization as it has done in Korea, Taiwan, and Indonesia. November 12, 2010, conference, Harvard University.

13. Despite high per capita income, however, democracy has not yet been fully achieved in Singapore or Hong Kong. China's per capita income at $4,400 is more than Indonesia's, the Philippines', and Brazil's were at the time of transition. It is still, however, less than Saudi Arabia's or Kuwait's (which have not undergone a shift to democracy).

14. Quoted by Manjeet Pardesi in *India Review* (July–September 2007).

15. Because it is not regarded as good enough when compared with European cars.

16. Cited in Erich Weede, "The Rise of India: Overcoming Caste Society and Permit-License-Quota Raj, Implementing Some Economic Freedom," *Asian Journal of Political Science* (August 2010): 131.

17. Quoted in Bill Emmott, *Rivals: How the Power Struggle Between China, India, and Japan Will Shape Our Next Decade* (Orlando, Fla.: Harcourt, 2008), p. 106.

18. The Association of Southeast Asian Nations (ASEAN) originally included Thailand, Malaysia, the Philippines, Indonesia, and Singapore. Burma, Vietnam, Brunei, Cambodia, and Laos have since been added. ASEAN + Three includes Japan, China, and South Korea. Asia-Pacific Economic Cooperation (APEC) is an unwieldy organization that, like the U.N. General Assembly, lumps nations together from many continents. It includes twenty-one members: Australia, Brunei, Canada, Chile, China, Hong Kong, Indonesia, Japan, the Republic of Korea, Malaysia, Mexico, New Zealand, Papua New Guinea, Peru, the Philippines, Russia, Singapore, Chinese Taipei (Taiwan), Thailand, the United States, and Vietnam.

CHAPTER 3. THE DECLINE AND RESURGENCE OF THE WEST

1. See Richard Morse, "The Heritage of Latin America," in Louis Hartz, *The Founding of New Societies: Studies in the History of the United States, Latin America, South Africa, Canada, and Australia* (New York: Harcourt, Brace and World, 1964), pp. 124–25.

2. See Louis Hartz, *The Liberal Tradition in America: An Interpretation of American Political Thought Since the Revolution* (New York: Harcourt, Brace, 1955).

3. Gouverneur Morris wrote: "They want an American constitution without realizing they have no Americans to uphold it." Quoted in ibid., p. 38.

4. As for manhood suffrage, "France reconfirmed it in 1875, England effected it in three stages between 1867 and 1918, Germany in 1871, and Italy in 1912." Arno J. Mayer, *The Persistence of the Old Regime: Europe to the Great War* (New York: Pantheon, 1981), p. 163.

5. Ibid., passim.

6. See Lewis Mumford, *Technics and Civilization* (Chicago: University of Chicago Press, 1934).

7. Personal communication but see also Robert Mundell, "The Euro and the Stability of the International Monetary System," paper presented at a conference on the euro as a stabilizer in the international economic system, December 1–3, 1998, Luxembourg. Luxembourg Institute for European and

International Studies and the Pierre Werner Foundation (Columbia University, January 1999).

8. See Glyn Morgan, *The Idea of a European Superstate: Public Justification and European Integration* (Princeton, N.J.: Princeton University Press, 2007).

9. See, for example, the work of Nouriel Roubini in *The Financial Times*.

10. Halford J. Mackinder, "The Geographic Pivot of History," *The Geographic Journal*, Royal Geographical Society (April 1904), p. 435.

11. Nicholas J. Spykman and Helen R. Nicholl, *The Geography of the Peace* (Hamden, Conn.: Archon, 1969).

12. Clyde Prestowitz, *Three Billion New Capitalists* (New York: Basic, 2005), p. 244. The figures in parenthesis are updated.

13. Gunter Verheugen was the E.U. official who masterminded this great expansion of Europe. Verheugen was not proud of being German. But he was proud of the European enlargement that took place in 2004 when he shepherded ten new countries into the European Union. This created the world's largest single market and reaffirmed Europe's acceptance of outside countries.

14. See Alkuin Kolliker, "Bringing Together or Driving Apart the Union? Towards a Theory of Differentiated Integration," *West European Politics* 24, no. 4 (October 2001). Kolliker writes: "Flexible arrangements with strong centripetal effects may lead to the eventual participation of most or all members, and therewith to the establishment of long-run unity at the relatively high level of integration chosen by the most willing members" (p. 126).

15. A public good is a benefit which, once created, extends to outsiders. A club good, in contrast, is a benefit confined to members.

16. See Stephen Walt, *The Origins of Alliances* (Ithaca, N.Y.: Cornell University Press, 1987). According to Walt: "States balance against the states that pose the greatest threat, and the latter need not be the most powerful states in the system." Furthermore he adds: "Whereas balance of power theory predicts that states will react to imbalances of power, balance of threat theory predicts that when there is an imbalance of threat (i.e., when one state or coalition appears especially dangerous), states will form alliances or increase their internal efforts in order to reduce their vulnerability" (p. 263).

17. Stephen Toulmin, *Cosmopolis* (Chicago: University of Chicago Press, 1992), p. 208.

18. Sometimes with help from the International Monetary Fund.

19. Charles Tilly concluded that wars increased administrative capacity among European states in the seventeenth century. Administrative, transport, and travel services may have done so in the Shogun's Japan. See Tilly, "War

Making and State Making as Organized Crime," in *Bringing the State Back In*, ed. Peter Evans, Dietrich Reuschemeyer, and Theda Skocpol (Cambridge: Cambridge University Press, 1985).

20. See Mayumi Fukushima, Richard Rosecrance, and Yuzuru Tsujyama, "Rising Sun in the New West," *The American Interest* 7 (May–June 2012).

21. See Francis Fukuyama, *Trust: The Social Virtues and the Creation of Prosperity* (New York: Simon and Schuster, 1996), p. 163.

22. One recent analysis explains: "One of the greatest benefits of the automotive keiretsu organization is the protection of the firm from market failure and the mitigation of financial risks. The keiretsu alliance of inter-firm agreements also contributes to lowering transaction costs such as coordinating costs, risks of broken contracts, searching costs, switching costs and product quality tests in imperfect markets. It has been proven that Japanese automotive chains incur less transaction costs than those in the US." Norifumi Kawai, "Shifting Gears: Keiretsu Corporate Networks Are Innate to the Japanese Auto Sector, but Could This System Finally Be Changing?" *Japan Inc.* 85 (Spring 2009): 10.

23. See Hartz, *The Liberal Tradition in America*.

24. John Quincy Adams became president in 1825 and Rutherford B. Hayes in 1877.

25. See Anthony Downs, *An Economic Theory of Democracy* (New York: Harper, 1957).

26. *New York Times*, September 4, 2011, p. 6.

27. Reich writes: "Even the executive class has an enlightened self interest in reversing the trend [to greater inequality]; just as a rising tide lifts all boats, the ebbing tide is now threatening to beach many of the yachts" (p. 6).

28. See Thomas L. Friedman and Michael Mandelbaum, *That Used to Be Us: What Went Wrong with America and How It Can Come Back* (London: Little Brown, 2011).

29. Zocalo Public Square, April 1, 2012.

30. Pew Research Center, March–April 2011.

31. See Wang Jisi and Kenneth Lieberthal, Brookings paper (2011). See also Cui Liru, "Peaceful Rise: China's Modernisation Trajectory," *Quarterly Journal of International Affairs (Istituto Affari Internazionali)* 47, no. 2, special issue, *A Rising China and Its Strategic Impact* (June 2012).

32. See the work of Rade Drmanac, an expert on whole genome sequencing. He is investigating hybridization of genome sequencing to make the process quicker, more efficient, and less costly.

33. See P. Raimondos-Moller and Alan Woodland, "A Note on Two Elementary Propositions on Customs Unions," (2001).

34. "In 2005 trade across the Atlantic in goods alone amount to nearly half a trillion dollars, a record. Europeans bought $186 billion worth of American exports, four times what the Chinese bought from the United States and 23 times more than what the Indians bought. Similarly the European Union sold the United States 251 billion Euros in merchandise, five times what it sold China and 12 times what it sold India. But it is foreign investment that is the driving force in the transatlantic relationship. In 2005 European investment into the United States totaled $66 billion, an increase of more than $13 billion over 2004 levels. And over the first half of this decade European investment accounted for over 75 percent of total foreign direct investment into the United States. Over the same period Europe was the destination for over 57 percent of total outflows of US direct investment abroad. . . . For example in 2005, US investment in Belgium alone was four times US investment in China. US investment in France was greater than what US firms invested in all of India that year. And these investments have proven quite successful. American affiliates earned $106 billion in profits in Europe in 2005, while European affiliate earnings in the US reached nearly $77 billion." "Completing the Transatlantic Market," February 2007, Transatlantic Policy Network, Brussels and Washington, D.C., p. 8.

35. President Obama, quoted in the *Financial Times*, October 28, 2011, p. 11.

36. Henry Kissinger, *The Troubled Partnership: A Re-Appraisal of the Atlantic Alliance* (Garden City, N.Y.: Doubleday, 1966), p. 251. He adds: "The dynamic periods of Western history occurred when unity was forged from diversity. This is the task once again. The struggles for prestige and influence can be salutary if at some point they lead to a heightened sense of community. Conversely, fifty years from now, no one will care who was 'right' with respect to the issues that form the headlines of the day if in the process the West has torn itself to pieces" (p. 250).

37. Martin Jacques, *When China Rules the World: The End of the Western World and the Birth of a New Global Order* (New York: Penguin, 2009), p. 227.

38. Ibid., p. 419.

CHAPTER 4. THE UNIFICATION OF THE UNITED STATES AND THE INTEGRATION OF THE WEST

1. Robert Gordon writes: "Looking back on the long history of Europe falling behind the U.S. and then catching up, it is hard to avoid the conclusion that this topic has more to do with politics and history than with economics. The sources of U.S. advantage prior to 1913 center on its internal common market, an achievement of the Founding Fathers." Robert J. Gor-

don, "Two Centuries of Economic Growth: Europe Chasing the American Frontier," paper prepared for Economic History Workshop, National Bureau of Economic Research (NBER), Northwestern University, October 17, 2002, p. 38.

2. Barry Eichengreen and Andrea Boltho, "The Economic Impact of European Integration," Centre for Economic Policy Research (Discussion Paper), May 2008.

3. See Jack A. Goldstone, Eric P. Kaufmann, and Monica Toft, *Political Demography: How Population Changes Are Reshaping International Security and National Politics* (Boulder, Colo.: Paradigm, 2012). Mark L. Haas's essay, "America's Golden Years: U.S. Security in an Aging World," pp. 49–62, provides useful data here.

4. See the key work here by Jacob Viner, *The Customs Union Issue* (New York: Carnegie Endowment for International Peace, 1950).

5. For still higher estimates, see J. Antal, "Transatlantic Free Trade Agreement—Still a Live or Dead Concept in EU-US Relations?" *International Journal of Social Sciences and Humanity Studies* 3, no. 2 (2011): 287–93.

6. This would incorporate NAFTA in the bargain.

7. See Jacques Servan-Schreiber, *The American Challenge*, trans. Ronald Steel (New York: Atheneum, 1968).

8. Robert Gordon observes the catch-up of European to American productivity and writes: "As one European nation after another overtakes and moves past the US level of productivity, one might conjecture that in ten years conferences will be organized at American universities on 'the sources of European advantage.'" Gordon, "Two Centuries of Economic Growth," p. 39.

### CHAPTER 5. THE TRAUMA OF POWER TRANSITION

1. The thirteen historical episodes are: (1) When France challenged the Hapsburgs over territory in Italy in the early 1500s, war occurred. (2) Sweden challenged the Hapsburgs for hegemony in Germany during the Thirty Years War. (3) When Holland challenged Spain to get independence (1560–1609), war occurred. (4) When rising England challenged Holland (mid seventeenth century), it was by war (1650–64). (5) When Prussia challenged Austria, it led to a long war (1740–63) over Silesia and primacy in Germany. (6) When France challenged Britain a long struggle ensued (1770–83 and again in 1798–1815). France won the first but lost the second encounter. (7) When Prussia challenged the France of Napoleon III it led to war (1870–71). (8) When Germany challenged imperial Great Britain, it led to

war (1914–18). (9) When the United States challenged Britain before World War I, it did not lead to war. (10) When Germany challenged Russia it was by war (1941–45). (11) When Germany and Japan challenged the United States it was by war (1941–45). (12) When the Soviet Union challenged the United States and the West during the Cold War, it did not lead to war. (13) When Japan passed the Soviet Union economically in 1983, it did not lead to war.

2. In 1632 it appeared that the Swedish king had triumphed over the Catholics. At the battle of Lutzen, Gustavus Adolphus met his death but he succeeded in uniting the Protestant cause against Austria. His victory represented the zenith of Swedish power during the Thirty Years War.

3. In 1896 Britain conceded to America (and Grover Cleveland) on the Venezuelan boundary (with British Guiana). Britain also acquiesced in American plans to build the Panama Canal and in a much larger U.S. Navy.

4. See George Modelski's and Robert Gilpin's work here. George Modelski, "The Long Cycle of Global Politics and the Nation-State," *Comparative Studies in Society and History* 20, no. 2 (April 1978), and Robert Gilpin, *War and Change in World Politics* (Cambridge: Cambridge University Press, 1981).

5. The United States waited until 1917 to join World War I on the Anglo-French side.

6. An episode experienced by C. P. Fitzgerald, the renowned expert on China, in his public school.

7. Quoted in Paul Kennedy, "German World Policy and the Alliance Negotiations with England, 1897–1900," *The Journal of Modern World History* 45, no. 4 (December 1973): 618.

8. See Pauline R. Anderson, *The Background of Anti-English Feeling in Germany, 1890–1902* (Washington, D.C.: American University Press, 1939).

9. His discussions with Haldane were later quoted in the *New York Times*, January 2, 1918.

10. If the Royal Navy was not superior to any other fleet in the English Channel, the home islands of Britain could be invaded. Thus British naval officers recognized that the navy was the only instrument of British power in which the issue of national survival could be decided "in the course of an afternoon."

11. See here the work of Paul Schroeder, who depicts a series of alternative strategies for menaced states. Paul W. Schroder, "The Nineteenth Century System: Balance of Power or Political Equilibrium?" *The Review of International Studies* 15 (1989): 135–53.

12. See Robert Powell, *In the Shadow of Power: State and Strategies in International Politics* (Princeton, N.J.: Princeton University Press, 1999), and Glenn Snyder, *Alliance Politics* (Ithaca, N.Y.: Cornell University Press), p. 51.

13. John Arquilla, *Dubious Battles* (London, 1992), and R. Rosecrance

and Chih-cheng Lo, "Balancing Stability and War: The Mysterious Case of the Napoleonic International System," *International Studies Quarterly* 40, no. 4 (December 1996). There is a huge literature on why the balance of power does not routinely take place. See John Vasquez, "The Realist Paradigm and Degenerative Versus Progressive Research Programs: An Appraisal of Waltz's Balancing Proposition," *American Political Science Review* 91, no. 4 (December 1997): 899–912. See also J. Vasquez and Colin Elman, eds., *Realism and the Balancing of Power: A New Debate* (Saddle River, N.J.: Prentice-Hall, 2003). See also Richard Rosecrance, "Is There a Balance of Power?" in *Realism and the Balancing of Power*, ed. Vasquez and Elman.

14. See F. H. Hinsley, *Power and the Pursuit of Peace: Theory and Practice in the History of Relations Between States* (Cambridge: Cambridge University Press, 1963), and Paul W. Schroeder, "Balance of Power and Political Equilibrium: A Response," *The International History Review* 16, no. 4 (November 1994): 661–880.

15. As shown by British reaction to the threat of German action against France in 1875.

16. China's first aircraft carrier was scheduled to be ready in 2012.

17. See Niall Ferguson, *The Pity of War: Explaining World War I* (London: Allen Lane, 1998), particularly, "Alternatives to Armageddon."

CHAPTER 6. MARKET CLUSTERS AUGMENT SIZE

1. See Edward Leamer, "A Flat World, A Level Playing Field, A Small World After All, or None of the Above" (review of Thomas Friedman, *The World Is Flat*), UCLA paper, 2007.

2. The data here are from Pankaj Ghemawat, *World 3.0: Global Prosperity and How to Achieve It* (Boston: Harvard Business Review Press, 2011).

3. As we shall see below, China has established parts of an auto industry. But nowhere does it furnish all the elements of a production chain by itself.

4. See Karl W. Deutsch, *Nationalism and Social Communication: An Inquiry into the Foundations of Nationality* (Cambridge: MIT Press, 1954).

5. See W. Brian Arthur, *Increasing Returns and Path Dependence in the Economy* (Ann Arbor: University of Michigan Press, 1994), Paul Krugman, *Geography and Trade* (Cambridge: MIT Press, 1991), and Allen J. Scott, *Regions and the World Economy: The Coming Shape of Global Production, Competition, and Political Order* (Oxford: Oxford University Press, 1998).

6. See Shujie Yao, "To Reach Its Full Potential, China Must Create Its Own Brands," *Financial Times*, June 8, 2011, p. 11.

7. In Europe, financial and industrial services and capabilities are located

in a geographic and high-tech arc stretching from London to Frankfurt. And there is an equally powerful craft, industrial, and financial complex that forms a similar shape from Zurich to Milan.

8. See, inter alia, Leamer, "A Flat World."

9. Edward Glaeser, *Triumph of the City* (New York: Penguin, 2011), p. 248.

10. Ibid, p. 269.

11. Anthony J. Venables, "Shifts in Economic Geography and Their Causes," paper presented at the Federal Reserve Bank of Kansas City's Symposium on the New Economic Geography, Jackson Hole, Wyo., 2006, p. 9.

12. Shujie Yao in *Financial Times*, June 8, 2011, p. 11.

13. U.S. Chamber of Commerce, "Transatlantic Zero," 2011.

14. See *Financial Times*, April 26, 2011.

15. See Eric Hobsbawn, *The Age of Empire, 1875–1914* (New York: Pantheon, 1987), and Paul M. Kennedy, *The Rise and Fall of the Great Powers: Economic Change and Military Conflict from 1500 to 2000* (New York: Random House, 1987).

16. Stephen G. Brooks, *Producing Security: Multinational Corporations, Globalization, and the Changing Calculus of Conflict* (Princeton, N.J.: Princeton University Press, 2005), p. 216.

CHAPTER 7. THE PROBLEM OF CHINA

1. Jacques asserts: "China's own experience of race is unique. Although once comprised of countless races, China is now dominated by what the Chinese regard to be one race, the Han Chinese." Jacques, *When China Rules the World*, p. 265.

2. See Harry Eckstein, "The British Political System," in *Patterns of Government: The Major Political Systems of Europe*, ed. Samuel H. Beer and Adam Ulam (New York: Random House, 1962).

3. This does not mean that foreigners or Islamists may not try to do so. Note the attacks on the London Tube stations in July 2007.

4. See also Benedict Anderson, *Imagined Communities: Reflections on the Origin and Spread of Nationalism* (London: Versol, 1986).

5. Charles Tilly, "Reflections on the History of European State-Making," in *The Formation of National States in Western Europe*, ed. Charles Tilly (Princeton, N.J.: Princeton University Press, 1975), p. 42.

6. Quoted in Francis Fukuyama, *The Origins of Political Order: From Prehuman Times to the French Revolution* (New York: Farrar, Straus, and Giroux, 2011), p. 76.

7. Ibid., chapter 7.

8. See Etel Solingen, *Regional Orders at Century's Dawn: Global and Domestic Influences on Grand Strategy* (Princeton, N.J.: Princeton University Press, 1998).

9. Barry Eichengreen, Donghyun Park, and Kwanho Shin, "When Fast Growing Economies Slow Down: International Evidence and Implications for China," *NBER Working Paper* 16919 (March 2011), pp. 8–9.

10. See *Financial Times*, October 17, 2011, p. 10.

11. Susan Shirk, *China, Fragile Superpower: How China's Internal Politics Could Derail Its Peaceful Rise* (New York: Oxford University Press, 2007), p. 63.

12. Todd Hall, "Unfinished Stories: Power Transitions and National Narratives in China," Princeton-Harvard Consortium on China Studies, April 2010, p. 3.

### CHAPTER 8. ALTERNATIVES

1. Wang Jisi, "China's Search for a Grand Strategy: A Rising Great Power Finds Its Way," *Foreign Affairs* 90, no. 2 (March–April 2011): 68–79.

2. See Michael Beckley, "China's Century? Why America's Edge Will Endure," *International Security* 36, no. 3 (Winter 2011–12): 41–78.

3. See Eichengreen, Park, and Shin, "When Fast Growing Economies Slow Down."

4. Some countries not members of the European Union are members of NATO, like Albania and Croatia. These two are likely soon to become members of the European Union.

5. See John Maynard Keynes on the transfer problem in *The Economic Consequences of the Peace* (New York: Harcourt, Brace and Howe, 1920).

### CHAPTER 9. HOW THE WEST ATTRACTS CHINA AND THE WORLD

1. In the same way a "Western" Iran could be Islamized as Ayatollah Khomeini came to power.

2. See Eugen Weber, *Peasants into Frenchmen: The Modernization of Rural France, 1870–1914* (Stanford, Calif.: Stanford University Press, 1976).

3. See particularly Charles Doran, *The Politics of Assimilation* (Baltimore: Johns Hopkins University Press, 1971).

4. See Joseph Nye, *Peace in Parts: Integration and Conflict in Regional Organization* (Boston: Little, Brown, 1971).

# Acknowledgments

I have been directly helped or theoretically influenced by a wide range of assistants and colleagues over the years. Randi Purchia, Tony Goldner, and Oliver Melton provided perspectives and data on mergers. Yuzuru Tsuyama and Mayumi Fukushima helped my work on China and Japan. Luisita Cordero refined the data on industrial links between countries. Ezra Vogel, Tony Saich, Karl Kaiser, and Jan Zielonka lent needed perspective on Asia and Europe. Jeff Frankel, Carl Kaysen, and David Richards provided overviews of the international economy and the strategic relationship of nations. Diplomatic and intellectual historians Paul Schroeder, Frank Fukuyama, Charles Maier, and Graham Allison suggested contrasting patterns that have determined outcomes among nations in past ages: where international economic and political relations can go in future is the primary subject of this book. Domestic politics represents an important variable, and John Owen IV and Archon Fung have taught me about its evolution over time.

## Acknowledgments

Zara Steiner and Niall Ferguson have influenced my understanding of present history. Steve Miller, Steve Walt, and Sean Lynn-Jones have indulged the evolution of my views about the "Size of the State" question over the past several years with good humor, and Wang Jisi, Jia Qingguo, and Tung Chee Hwa have tried to set me right on China. Emma Belcher, Etel Solingen, and Jim Sebenius convinced me that an agglomeration of countries was still possible if sought in the right way. I am indebted to Alan Alexandroff and Art Stein for many comments and criticisms over the years. Bill Frucht skillfully clarified the text. My greatest debt is to Barbara Rosecrance, who reviewed, rewrote, and polished most of what follows. She refused, however, to be listed as co-author.

# Index

# Index

# Index

## Index

# Index

# Index

*Index*